KASHMIR

R.Indus

Simla

Ambala

Patiala

rnal

Badli-
ke-serai

Delhi

Meerut

ROHILKHAND

HIMALAYA MOUNTAINS

NEPAL

Bareilly

Shah
Jahanpur

Aligarh

Fatehgarh

Sitapur

OUDH

Agra

Lucknow

Unao

Faizabad

Gwalior

Cawnpore

Kalpi

Azamgarh

Kunch

Fatehpur

R.Ganges

Patna

R.Ganges

R.Jumna

R.Jumna

Benares

Dinapur

Jhansi

Allahabad

BEHAR

Rahatgarh

Saugur

The
Indian Mutiny

The British
at War

General Editor:
Ludovic Kennedy

John Harris

The
Indian Mutiny

Book Club Associates London

This edition published 1973 by
Book Club Associates
By arrangement with Granada Publishing Ltd

Copyright © 1973 by Hubert Cole

ISBN 0 246 10618 2
Filmset by Keyspools Ltd, Golborne, Lancs.
Printed in Great Britain by
C. Tinling & Co Ltd, Prescot & London.

Contents

Acknowledgements

The photographs and illustrations in this book are reproduced by kind permission of the following. The portrait on page 17 by the gracious permission of H M the Queen. Those on pages 13, 23, 24, 29, 34, 35, 36, 38, 43, 53, 66, 86, 87, 88, 89, 92, 121, 122, 124, 137, 138, 164, 168, 169, 176, 188 and 189, National Army Museum; pages 45, 50, 82, 103, 115, 152, 158, 190, 193 and 196, Victoria and Albert Museum; pages 8, 14, 46–7, 56, 57, 59, 78, 116, 149 and 163, India Office Library and Records; pages 10, 61, 111, 126 and 150, National Portrait Gallery; pages 32, 42, 49, 71, 72, 76, 84, 90, 104, 105, 107, 109, 112, 130, 132, 143, 144, 147, 157, 172–3, 174, 194 and 201, Radio Times Hulton Picture Library; pages 37, 40 and 154–5, Mansell Collection; pages 54, 127, 129 and 204, The Parker Gallery; pages 182–3 and 178–9, Trustees of the Tate Gallery; page 96, Trustees of the British Museum; pages 139, 140 and 187, Queen's Own Highlanders (Seaforth and Camerons); page 184, Queen's Dragoon Guards; page 75, Queen's Lancashire Regiment; page 70, Sherwood Foresters Museum; page 69, Somerset Light Infantry Museum; page 19, Congregational Council for World Mission; page 181, Sheffield City Art Galleries; page 18, Mr Michael Appleby: the pictures on pages 166 and 167 are from *Recollections of a Winter Campaign in India 1857–1858* by Capt. Oliver Jones, RN; on page 31, from *Curry and Rice* by G. F. Atkinson; and on page 101 from *Campaign in India* also by G. F. Atkinson. Illustration Research Service provided the pictures. The maps were drawn by Brian and Constance Dear.

Introduction

The great Indian Mutiny of 1857 is remembered for events that
have become legendary; the massacre at Cawnpore; the Kashmir
Gate at Delhi; the relief of Lucknow. In this book John Harris has
vividly brought to life the pity and terror of the Mutiny, the sense
of shock to both sides at the challenge to established order.
Britishers in India and England were horrified by the murders of
women and children, and yet British reprisals were no less horrific;
captured rebel sepoys were blown from guns. Despite its horrors
the Mutiny was followed by one of the most splendid chapters in
British Imperial History – the long years of the Raj. Yet looking
back, we can see that in that year of 1857 – when a coloured people
rose against its British rulers for the first time – were the first
stirrings of the movement that was to lead to independence in 1947,
and eventually to the dissolution of the Empire itself.

Ludovic Kennedy

Chapter 1

Men
on Stilts

In May 1857, Queen Victoria's England seemed at peace. The Crimean War, recently over, had shown up the defects of a moribund army system but attempts were now being made to put things right, and it was believed that Britain's good name held everywhere and that prosperity was on the increase. British dominions overseas seemed secure in Africa, Canada, New Zealand, Australia, and a host of other places.

Not least important among them was India, where Robert Clive and the young men of the East India Company had wrenched a continent from the hands of its native princes and presented it to Britain as a vast and priceless jewel which was to enrich her for generations.

It was one hundred years since Clive had taken India from the French and, though most of the British were unaware of it, an old prophecy stated that in this centenary year of the Battle of Plassey their hold would crumble. The East India Company had long ceased to be merely the trading organisation that had been given power in India in the days of Elizabeth I, and its strength had grown so that, though its right to trade had been surrendered, it had become, in fact, the British Government's representative on the sub-continent. Through its agents and tax-collectors and the Governor-General, Lord Canning, it held control from the Himalayas to the southernmost tip. As the power of the Moghul emperors had declined, the Indian princes, both Hindu and Moslem, had become merely its puppets.

It had taken the Indians a long time to realise that they were no longer masters in their own country. Because the Company had originally acted in the name of the princes, the fact that power had been captured by a foreign race had not at first been apparent. But slowly, as the Company's agents behaved with considerably less dignity and honesty than the agents of the Crown would have done, the Indians began to wake up and the realisation became widespread. Perhaps the Company's decision in 1835 to strike coins from which the last Moghul emperor's name was omitted, was one of the first things that made people aware of what had happened and even as early as 1837 shrewd administrators were beginning to notice a change. Although outwardly everything was calm, and though the peasant, the industrialist, the trader and the oppressed felt the British had brought undreamt-of blessings, the situation had in fact become 'charged with dynamite'.

It was an age of reform and the British wished to reform India – even as they conquered it – both politically and morally. While

Opposite
Even the most junior officer or official in India had a host of servants.

9

Clive had used Indian forms of government to disguise the true sources of power, Lord Canning's predecessor, Lord Dalhousie – at thirty-five the youngest-ever Governor-General – had thought differently. He believed that India under the British was happier than India under its native rulers – many of whom were descended, anyway, from comparatively recent soldiers-of-fortune – and, exploiting an old Indian law, he had therefore removed many of the feudal states and kept only a few of the larger ones, under the control of the Central Government.

In itself, it was not a bad idea, because it would have led eventually to better government, but Dalhousie's methods had been ruthless. At first he had annexed states where there was no direct heir, because the constant discord had brought misery. But for the same reason he had also refused to accept that a childless ruler had the right to adopt an heir, and many minor states such as Satara, Jhansi and Nagpur were annexed, as well as the property of those landlords who could produce no proper title to their estates. His final and most dangerous seizure was that of the Muslim kingdom of Oudh, where his excuse was its gross mismanagement. The annexation had stirred the resentment of Muslims all over India. Though the king was given a pension and allowed to live in luxury, those who depended on him for a living or a comfortable old age – even the peasants whose lands were part of his domains – were not considered at all. In addition, Coverly Jackson, the man placed in charge, was a tactless, unsympathetic man surrounded by incompetent subordinates.

The British had done a lot of good, but they had also unwittingly done a lot of harm. *Suttee* (widow-burning), infanticide and thuggism, practices which were abhorrent even to enlightened Indians, had been suppressed, but the Indian masses regarded the suppression as interference in their way of life. And the Company was always too greedy. While its expenditure for the good of India remained small, its taxes fell heavily, not only on the wealthy, but also on the poor. Tolls had to be paid to cross rivers, and salt – so essential in the tropics – was a government monopoly. Liquor and opium were also beyond the reach of the poor, and even those native princes and landowners who had still not been touched, waking up at last to the fact that Dalhousie had already annexed over 250,000 square miles of India, began to grow afraid. It would be their turn next, they decided, as they saw the British apparently seeking to change the very structure of Indian social and political life. Unfortunately, there was no means by which either side could put its point of view because there was no body on which the representatives of the Company could meet representatives of the Indians; as a result, the British were never in a position to sense the outrage their subjects felt against them.

Nevertheless, on 10 May 1857, all seemed well. Though the hot weather was near, it was mild still and, with the sun reaching its zenith, for those who could leave the most important thing in their minds was the coming journey to the hills where they could pass the hot season. For the rest, the sweltering heat of the plains meant spending as much time as possible in shuttered houses with only the slow wafting of the punkah to move the air. The shimmering afternoon had emptied of white men and only a few natives were visible, dozing in the shade like bundles of old rags. India seemed ancient and quiet and at peace.

Lord Canning, Governor-General of India, on whom the fury of the Mutiny fell.

Beneath the dark surface, however, mutterings were taking place. Canning was not unaware of them. '. . . In the sky of India,' he had said at the farewell dinner given to him in London before he had left, '. . . . a small cloud may rise, at first no bigger than a man's hand but which . . . may at last threaten to overwhelm us with ruin.' His words had surprised his audience but, in fact, they seemed later to be prophetically inspired because messages were already being passed and cabalistic symbols scrawled on walls, and the British were only hours away from an era of sweat, tears, torment and savage atrocity. To some it was to mean massacre and mutilation, when women saw their husbands and children butchered before their eyes. To some, caught in besieged towns, it was to mean long periods of agonised waiting until relief came. To some it was to mean no more than the unbelievable shock and outrage of seeing men they had trusted turn on them. But to all of them, important and unimportant, civilian and soldier, male and female, it was to be a period of dread when the knowledge that violent death was probably not very far away was large in their minds. Often they were to struggle across burning plains or through steaming jungles, either in escape or in an effort to exact vengeance, and to many of them it was to mean the end of life, from exhaustion, heatstroke or one of the many diseases that plagued Asia.

Though the great years of trade, when a man could go to India as a clerk and return a nabob to set himself up in a vast country mansion in England, were past, John Company was still strong. The pioneering spirit – like the pioneering days – was gone, however, and the great epoch of Clive was over, and, with competition from the

French, Dutch and Portuguese overcome, the Company had ceased to be as efficient as it had been. Nepotism and corruption were rife, and though profits had slumped, there was still money to be made from the sale of salaried positions, while in India, for many functionaries the trappings had become almost more important than the duties. Vast official palaces – colonnaded and European in design – were built in the Company's three main centres and an aristocracy of officialdom had grown up among the well-connected who held the best jobs.

And as the Company had grown slothful, so its lesser officials and representatives in the hinterland, both civilian and military, had also fallen into bad habits. Struggling always to keep up the appearances of England, trying to be as English as possible, they, too, had often almost forgotten the reason for their existence there. They kept carefully to the shade, avoiding the fierce Indian sun, the women in sprigged muslin dresses, the soldiers in summer uniforms, the civilian administrators in the alpaca jackets which were the almost universal official garb in the heat. As cut off from England as if they were on another planet, their time was spent, largely in boredom, between their clubs and their homes, where they were waited on by hordes of attendants. Houses were built for coolness and, with servants and kitchen situated in a detached building, their furnishings were very much those of Victorian England, over-stuffed in a way that made them stifling, as their owners sought to reproduce in the heat of the sub-continent the gracious manners of the place they still called 'home'. Well-paid by European standards and far from overworked, they considered themselves secure, efficient and well able to hold India in thrall.

The truth was that things had changed and they were no longer as good as they had been or as good as they imagined they still were. All too often they were small men – men on stilts – reaching up beyond their capabilities. The standing of the British had begun to decrease when the country became more settled. Marriageable English girls began to pour in looking for husbands and more leave was taken, and the old habit of acquiring a mistress and learning the language and customs in bed disappeared. The new-type officer learned his Hindi from a text-book.

With the Englishwomen, many of them ardent writers of diaries and pious pillars of the Church, came a flood of missionaries, intolerant, dogmatic, fired by Victorian zeal and quoting the Old Testament more often than the New. Regarding the conversion of the whole country to Christianity as only a matter of time, they considered it 'ripe for the harvest' and they were everywhere,

12

not only in their churches but in the prisons, schools and market places. While the Indians did not object to their right to propagate their own religion, they found they were not content with explaining Christ but were also busy ridiculing rites and practices that had been common for generations in India.

For British officials the trappings became more important than the duties, and vast official palaces, like these in Calcutta, were built.

Claiming for Christianity a 'monopoly of truth', they regarded it as not only their vocation but also their positive duty to convert everyone with a dark skin. India was to be not only a jewel in the British Crown but also a Christian jewel. The country, they firmly believed, was being governed for the good of its inhabitants and Christianity was part of the idea; and concessions for Christian converts – such as allowing them to inherit property which as Hindus or Muslims they could not claim – had been allowed to creep in.

Moreover, the East India Company men who had all too often gone to India because their futures in England had not been bright and who now found themselves in positions of power, were full of racial pride; they treated the Indians, even noblemen and chieftains, with distaste, regarding their religion as barbaric. Their wives, as often as not, were even worse, viewing the Indians with the parochial imperiousness they had so often seen at home in the British aristocracy which they now tried to ape. With the affairs of the Company in the hands of such narrow-minded snobs and bigots, the links between the whites and the Indians began to weaken.

It was the same with the army. The army in India had grown originally from the simple necessity for the East India Company to guard the goods it bought and sold, and the step from armed guards to trained troops officered by Englishmen was inevitable. The num- 13

ber of British troops was never very large but the army, with its three main centres in the Bombay, Madras and Calcutta Presidencies, was able to recruit without trouble from the native Indians. Company regiments were raised under British officers with Indian officers serving under them – though the most senior Indian was always subordinate to the lowest-ranking Englishman. Most European troops were British regiments hired out to the Company for a tour of overseas duty, and with the British in the ratio of one to 4,000, the ratio of troops had been fixed by a former Governor-General as one British soldier to three native soldiers and had never been less than one to four. With the Crimean War draining off men, however, and trouble in Burma, China and Persia, the ratio had been allowed to become almost one to eight – 40,160 European troops as against 311,000 native troops, among whom were 5,362 British officers.

Originally, these native soldiers had been low-caste Afghan or Turkish mercenaries, but in an attempt to make the army more national, the sons of landowners and peasants had been deliberately recruited. In the army of Bengal, with its cantonments stretching along the Ganges and the Jumna from Calcutta to Peshawar, three-fifths of the men serving in the 63 infantry regiments came from Oudh, 'the nursery of soldiers'. As servants of the British in their home state, they had held a privileged position and were supported by the British against the corrupt native government, but with the annexation in 1856 these privileges had disappeared. From being important when they went home, the Oudh soldiers – already humiliated by the seizure of their homeland – had now begun to

14

find they were being treated there as nothing, or even with contempt as slaves of the British. Many of them were Brahmins, high-born Hindus, while the cavalry, who lived apart, were Muslims.

Well-paid by their own standards, they were popular with the British. Dressed in the same scarlet jackets and white cross-belts so that Indian opponents should not know where the line was European and where native, they looked the part with their curled beards and whiskers. They were enthusiastic, intelligent and able, and seemed to be loyal, though there had been previous instances of trouble among them. At Vellore in Southern India in 1806, for instance, the native soldiers, or sepoys, had revolted because they had been ordered to wear a new style of headdress which included a leather cockade believed to be made of cowhide or pigskin. With the cow sacred to the Hindu and the pig unclean to the Muslim, the cockade offended the religion of both and when they were also ordered to trim their beards and give up wearing their caste marks, they began to believe an attempt was being made to force them into becoming Christians and they rose during the night to murder their officers in their beds.

In 1824, a regiment ordered to go to Burma had refused because of a dispute over cooking pots and because they believed they were to be transported by sea, in defiance of their caste feelings. In both cases other influences had worked on the excitable, superstitious soldiers. In the first case Vellore was the home of the children of Tipu Sahib, the Sultan of Mysore, Wellington's old opponent, who were cherishing visions of a restoration of their dynasty and, in the second, reports of defeat in Burma led them to expect the end of the Company's authority. Both of these mutinies had been brutally suppressed and the ringleaders hanged, their bodies swinging in chains as an example to others, while hundreds had been condemned to years of hard labour on the roads. There had been more trouble after the wars of 1839 to 1849 when the accountants of the Company, to save money, had unwisely decided that allowances for service outside the soldier's native states must cease. It had caused hardship, and regiments – by this time linked by post – refused to move. When they won their point it began to dawn on them that there was power in unified action.

In 1852, when the 38th Native Infantry refused to cross the sea to Burma, where the British were again involved in a war of annexation, enlightened opinion demanded that this mutiny should be resolved simply by a change of station; but in 1856 the General Service Enlistment Act was brought in to give the authorities absolute power to take the soldiers out of India. To cross the *Kala*

Pani, the black waters, was pollution to an orthodox Hindu and reduced him in caste, and no Indian soldier could eat salt pork or ship's biscuit. The whole of Northern India was uneasy and it was obvious to the sepoys that, although the Indian troops took all the rough and ordinary duties of the service, more than half the money spent on the army went on the small proportion of British.

Even in the British regiments all was far from well. Purchase, the system by which officers obtained their commissions, all too often resulted in a wholesale changeover of officers when a regiment went abroad. Those with money remained in England, going on half-pay or buying into a different regiment, while their places were taken by men who would otherwise never have got commissions. The senior captain of the 61st (Queen's) Foot, who had been unable to get a commission in England, was five feet two inches tall, with an enormous head, short, hunch-backed body, long arms, and thin, shrivelled legs. Marching, he was unable to keep step with his men and on horseback looked 'more like a monkey than a human being'.

Yet, well aware that so long as they had a little money they could still get promotion, they did not have to worry about their commanders' disapproval and officers formed their own ideas about how much work they should do. Even the most conscientious did little more than an hour's duty a day in the hot weather. It was believed that exposure to the sun might be fatal, so the European officers rarely made an appearance except in the morning or evening. During the rest of the daylight hours they remained in their darkened shabby bungalows, bored, underpaid, frustrated, and often drinking far too much.

Sir William Mansfield, later Lord Sandhurst, Commander-in-Chief, India, noticed that they were often not as zealous or as smart as a commanding officer had a right to expect and that their fibre and behaviour had often been sapped by heat, liquor, idleness and supercession. Aften ten years on the sub-continent, he claimed, they

were often physically or morally weaker, 'less amenable to discipline . . . more slothful, and . . . incapable of prolonged effort.'

With the officers of the Company's army, the situation was probably even worse. In the past, impoverished men, seeking a fortune, had gone eagerly to the East to face an exile of perhaps thirty years and as often as not had died without returning home or even expecting to. They had therefore made their lives with their regiments, identifying themselves entirely with their men, speaking their language and taking Indian 'wives'. But now they had grown indifferent and lacking in zeal and the generals were old and unfit,

Missionaries, fired by Victorian zeal, were everywhere in India.

and inactive because of long service in bad climates. They did not like responsibility or anything that involved giving up their comforts, and had lost the gift of making quick decisions.

Their juniors were often not a great deal better. Subalterns – though inevitably there were brilliant exceptions – were all too often concerned with a life of luxury and ease, and General John Jacob had long since noticed a lamentable lack of high moral tone and traditional Anglo-Saxon honesty among them as they maintained their huge staffs of menials. Because of the sun, they had taken to travelling in litters or covered carriages instead of on horseback and had to be kept cool at all times with a punkah; even the most junior among them had to have a host of servants – 'one for his pipe, another for his umbrella, another for his bottle, another for his chair, etc., all to do the work of one man.' Even a white private soldier could not draw his own water or cook his own victuals, and the life of luxury inevitably ended in debt – a state which in itself was regarded by Indians with contempt. Subalterns often did not hesitate to show their dislike of their men – 'I hate the natives', they said, or 'I like to beat a black fellow' – and were sometimes even slapdash enough for their men to despise them and show their feelings without hesitation. In no way did they set that example which was more necessary for discipline in an army of mixed creeds and languages than punishment.

As was common in Victorian armies, too, it was usual for an officer to take long periods of leave, either for business or personal reasons and, in addition, the best – the most vigorous and intelligent

Opposite
General Sir John Hearsey, in the uniform of the 2nd Bengal Irregular Cavalry of East India Company Army.

19

– were snatched away for the civil or political posts which had been created by the Government's wholesale annexation of land. Half the officers of the Bengal army were away from their regiments for much of their service – on duty, on business, or on furlough in the hills – and, with regiments constantly chopping and changing, they sometimes had as many as four different commanders in a year. The young officer remaining with his men became known as a failure. Otherwise, it was felt, he would have been taken away to govern a province. Sir Charles Napier, the conqueror of Sind, had noticed that regiments were often commanded by lieutenants and prophesied that one day they would find the army taken out of their hands by high-caste Indians of intelligence and daring.

Due to interference from headquarters, the Bengal army was not even as good as the other two, and had been called 'the most expensive and inefficient in the world.' In a high-caste organisation like that of Bengal, where the British commanded Brahmins of strong religious beliefs, they needed to be much more alert and aware than they were. There were whole battalions who were vegetarians, and men who would follow a British officer anywhere or rescue him in the teeth of fire, would rather starve than eat from a cooking pot on which his shadow had fallen. In the middle of the morning march it was necessary to allow such men to remove their belts, boots and accoutrements and light 700 separate little cooking fires to cook 1,400 separate little cakes of wheat. The rules for the Rajputs who made up the major portion of the rest of the army were only slightly less complicated.

It had always been possible for good officers to persuade them all – Brahmin, Rajput and Muslim – to forget in an emergency many of these ritual absurdities, but with peace and idleness such store was set by them they seemed to be necessary to salvation. And with the British officer and Indian soldier each tending to regard the other's faith and personal habits as faintly disgusting, the set-up inevitably created difficulties for those Indian NCOs who happened to be of a different caste. To exacerbate the problem, many of these men were old and had lost their first keenness, because the Bengal army's methods of promotion – different from those of the Madras and Bombay armies – depended on age more than skill, and often pensions were refused while a man could still put one foot before another. Useless, worn-out men, sent back to commanding officers by the invaliding committees, had long been a nuisance and a source of discontent in the camps.

Even the best of the commanding officers found their job impossible. They had no real power themselves and the Government had also reduced the power of the white officers who should have backed them up, particularly with regard to punishment. In India the wages of sin had always been swift and barbaric but, with the weight of enlightened Christian opinion making itself felt, decisions on matters of life and death were no longer left in the hands of commanding officers. The avenging sword was now sometimes a matter of six hundred miles away and native officers, punished by their commanders, appealed to the Commander-in-Chief. Frequently they found themselves reinstated and returned to their regiment, laughing not only at their commanding officer for his lack of power but at the man hundreds of miles away who had changed the sentence, for his weakness. Commanders who had once seemed all-powerful came to be regarded as mere cogs in a great wheel and sepoys even started to make frivolous complaints, knowing perfectly well that their officers could do nothing about them. Discipline slipped. Sepoys straggled on the march and, dismissed from parade, tore off their uniforms and wore linen drawers which in some regiments were even worn on guard. Old soldiers blamed a former Governor-General, Lord William Bentinck, who had abolished corporal punishment for the Indian army twenty years before. The army, they claimed, had ceased to fear.

Even pride in their achievements had disappeared. Though the great wars in India, when the warlike Sikhs had been brought under subjection, were still in the memory, there had been disasters as well as victories. In Kabul in 1842, due to British inefficiency, sixteen thousand British and Indian troops and their dependants had been besieged and then massacred by the Afghans, so that only a single survivor, Dr William Brydon, had ridden in to Jallalabad to bring the news. At Mudki the British had allowed themselves to be surprised, and though the victories at Ferozeshah and Aliwal had been notable there had been high casualties, while Chilianwallah had been only a series of blunders. Looking back at them, the Indians had come to realise that the British were not invincible against Asiatics, and the disasters of the Crimean War had sent British prestige to rock bottom.

As with the British, the Indian character had also sunk low. Even among those who saw in the situation the chance of ousting their conquerors there was never much agreement and a great deal of jealousy, intrigue and personal ambition. While the sudden and explosive outbreak of the Mutiny led the British to believe it had been planned, in fact there was no real conspiracy. Nevertheless ideas had been discussed by discontented men in dusty palaces and chief among the talkers were Ahmed Abdullah, the Maulavi of 21

Faizabad, adviser to the ex-king of Oudh; the Rani of Jhansi, an intelligent, courageous woman, bitter at the seizure of her state; Dondhu Pant, the Rajah of Bithur, better known as the Nana Sahib; and other Mahratta and Moghul supporters. The Maulavi, in particular – like the Nana Sahib – had been active for some time. A tall, lean, muscular man with deep-set eyes and a high aquiline nose, he was a prime mover in the discontent. After the annexation of Oudh, he had travelled over the North-West Provinces on a mission that remained a mystery to the British authorities and had visited Delhi, Meerut, Patna and Calcutta, and on his return had circulated seditious papers in Oudh. He had actually been apprehended at Lucknow when the Mutiny freed him. Such men as he were naturally in touch with the discontented sepoys.

There were still a few Englishmen with their eyes open and their ears to the ground, however. Charles Metcalfe, son of a British Resident at Delhi, expected to wake one morning to find the whole of India lost to the English Crown, while at Barrackpore, General Sir John Hearsey, the Divisional Commander, was of the opinion that they were 'dwelling on a mine ready for explosion'. For safety Lord Canning, who had replaced Lord Dalhousie as Governor-General, had rescued from exile in Rajputana Sir Henry Lawrence – a man disliked by Dalhousie – whom he made Chief Commissioner for Oudh in place of the tactless Jackson in March 1857.

The increased ratio of Indian troops to British troops, which might not have been important at any other time, suddenly began to matter as the Indians' confidence in John Company and the army dwindled. Small mutinies or near-mutinies took place, the first rifts of hatred between white and coloured people. Almost all of them were caused by the fear that the British were trying to break caste and force the sepoys into Christianity, and the pattern was always the same and always seemed to start outside the regiment. Men returning from leave brought news of a bad harvest or a heavy tax assessment, to be followed by the rumour that all the Company's armies had been killed in Burma and all the British in the Crimea. Other rumours came behind them, so silly at times that under any other conditions no one would have listened to them. Englishwomen, it was said, were to be brought to India to marry Indian princes whose children would then become Christians and all sepoys would be baptised. There was to be a mass murder of sepoys by a mine under the parade ground. The British had polluted the sugar and mixed ground bullocks' bones with the flour, and the sepoys were to be forced to eat cow's flesh. Invariably there was
22 maliciousness behind them, usually dispensed by some dispossessed

landowner or his agent, but though the Government heard the stories as much as the sepoys, they did little to discount them. Ignoring the fact that their Indian soldiers regarded service in the form of a trade guild in which son followed father in the handling of weapons, they continued high-handedly to disregard their customs and religions.

Though outwardly all remained calm and the Indians seemed loyal, below the surface it was a highly inflammable situation and all it required to cause it to burst into flame was some common cause to unite the diversified religions. According to the Indian historian, Surendra Nath Sen, the Hindu-Muslim problem which continued to plague India to the end of British rule, had never existed before their arrival and, despite their differences, there had been a friendly relationship between men of the different religions based on the common life of centuries. However, since it *had* arisen, the British had not discouraged it, feeling they were secure as long as the Hindus and the Muslims distrusted each other. But now, as it was decided to replace the old heavy Brown Bess smooth-bore musket, with which most of the Company's army was equipped, with the new Enfield rifle which had proved so effective in the Crimea, the two sects at last found the one thing that could effectively unite them once more in their dislike of the British.

To load the new rifle entailed extracting from a pouch a cartridge with a greased patch at the top which was torn off with the teeth and then used to assist in ramming the bullet down the barrel. This was something British soldiers, even those Indian soldiers who had experimented with the new weapon, had done without the slightest hesitation, but now the sepoys began to believe – with some reason – that the grease was made from the fat of a cow or the fat of a pig. To both Hindu and Muslim the grease would have been an abomination for which there is no parallel in European ways of thinking, and once again, the sepoys saw it as an attempt to break their caste and force them to become Christians. At first slowly, then, as the stories were spread by agitators, with increasing anger, the Indian regiments refused to accept the cartridge.

Left A musket used at the time of the Indian Mutiny.

Right Torradas musket.

23

Chapter 2

Outbreak
at Meerut

The first indication that the new cartridges were an insult to caste came in January 1857, at Dum Dum, near Calcutta, where they were prepared. A lascar – one of the lowest of castes – who was employed in their manufacture, asked a high-caste Brahmin sepoy for a drink from his brass bowl. When indignantly refused he just as indignantly retorted that the sepoy had no reason to be fussy as his caste would soon be defiled anyway, because the grease on the new cartridges he used was a mixture of cow fat and hog fat. Appalled, the soldier hurried back to barracks with the story and, because the soil was favourable, it spread like wildfire as regiments, remembering the advantages of the post, began to correspond with each other.

It was not really the cartridge that had done the trick, however. 'A consciousness of power', it was said after it was all over, 'had grown up in the army which could only be exorcised by mutiny', and if it had not been the cartridge some other excuse would inevitably have been found.

In fact, so far, none of the cartridges had yet been generally issued. Advised of the problems, the Commander-in-Chief, India, General the Honourable George Anson, had ordered that they were to be issued ungreased. It was already too late, however, and in one station after another the sepoys 'respectfully but firmly' refused to touch them. The days when the sepoys admired their officers were now past and they were sullen and lacking in trust. A few officers of tact and courage, like General Hearsey at Barrackpore, who spoke the sepoys' language, were sympathetic and tried to explain that no attempt was being made to interfere with their religions; but, unfortunately, even as they spoke, their words were being contradicted by those British who believed it was their duty to preach Christianity.

The fervour of religion was strong in mid-Victorian England, and it increased rather than diminished in a country of alien creeds. The Commissioner at Fatehpur put up at his own expense four pillars at each entrance to the city inscribed in Urdu and Hindi with the Ten Commandments, while one of Hearsey's own senior officers, Colonel Wheler, of the 34th Native Infantry, made no secret of the fact that he had preached the Gospel to his men for twenty years and that his avowed intention – 'the aim and end of every Christian who speaks the word of God' – was to convert them to Christianity.

The tension built up to an ugly situation. Strange stories began to be heard as barracks were mysteriously burned and bungalows

25

were set ablaze by flaming arrows fired, it was said, by soldiers. Then a new report came in from Delhi of flat cakes of flour known as *chupattis* being passed from village to village south of the city, like the fiery cross in the Highlands of Scotland. Incantations were being murmured as the *chupattis* were handed over and new information spoke of them now nearly three hundred miles away, travelling swiftly in an ever-widening circle. Somehow they were unnerving and seemed to suggest a well-organised scheme for passing messages, for surely the cakes had some meaning. To this day, however, no clue has been found to indicate what was behind them. They were probably nothing more than a propitiation of the Gods against disaster or because a business had failed but a few officials, seeing a more sinister meaning, suspected they were the symbols of rebellion. When questioned, the Indians feigned ignorance or said quite honestly that they believed the British Government had ordered it all.

There was clearly something in the wind, however; signs began to appear on walls, and rumours of the horrors the British had in mind for them were spread among the soldiers who looked around and saw whole districts administered by a solitary official. They knew well that if only the Indians could be persuaded to act together they could sweep the British into the sea, and warnings of the coming whirlwind shifted uneasily through the bazaars. General Hearsey and others warned against the use of the greased cartridges which seemed to be causing so much anger and distress, and suggested that the matter might be overcome by allowing the sepoys to make their own grease. They were overruled by the Adjutant-General who felt it might make the sepoys think that old cartridges covered with an inoffensive fat which they had been using for some time were also contaminated. On his advice, Canning decided that concession would be weakness and, refusing to give in to what he considered the prejudices of his soldiers, he ordered the cartridges to be used.

Those British officers who understood their men were appalled. Captain Edward Martineau, musketry instructor at Ambala, angrily pointed out to a member of Anson's staff that the order had produced 'all the elements of combustion', and loyal servants began to drop hints of sepoys meeting to plot mutiny. These were passed on to Anson but nothing was done and he did not think it worth while to make a single representation about them to the authorities.

The truth was that as early as 26 February, the 19th Native Infantry at Berhampur had refused the cartridge and had been marched to Barrackpore to be disbanded under the eyes of a British regiment specially brought back from Burma – a fact which was rightly construed by the agitators as an indication of how thin on the ground the white soldiers were. The sepoys' arrival had provoked another incipient mutiny. On 29 March, a young soldier of Wheler's 34th called Mangal Pande, affected by the heat and drugs and believing that the British were about to turn against the native soldiers, ran amok and fired at his British adjutant and sergeant-major, calling on his comrades to join him. The guard did not join in but they did not disarm him either and, drawing his sword, he wounded both the Englishmen who were also struck by the guards with their muskets. Wheler did little to regain control and only when General Hearsey appeared was the uproar put down. Warned of Mangal Pande's loaded musket, Hearsey snorted 'Damn his musket!' and clapped spurs to his horse. The old man's simple courage was sufficient to end the incipient mutiny. Driving up to the guard, the battle-worn, sixty-year-old general waved his revolver. 'The first man who refuses to march when I give the word is a dead man', he roared, and the guard submitted and followed him. Seeing them approach, Mangal Pande lost his nerve and attempted to shoot himself. He failed and was hanged, as was the native officer in command of the guard.

Because the British officers of the 34th believed the incident to be an isolated one, however, nothing was immediately done about the regiment. Canning was busy writing elegant minutes, worrying about details and devising ways to coax the sepoys into accepting the cartridges, and when the news was flashed to him by the newly-instituted electric telegraph, such was the poor quality of the advice he received, that it was decided to disband the 34th without punishment and even pay their passages home. By this time, however, disbandment was no punishment at all because there was hardly a native regiment in the Bengal Presidency which was not ready to disband itself and turn on its officers. Signs of unrest were also showing in the 48th Native Infantry at Lucknow whose regimental surgeon, Dr Wells, feeling unwell, had unthinkingly drunk from a medicine bottle, forgetting that he had thus hopelessly polluted it in the eyes of his Hindu patients. On hearing the complaints, the colonel of the regiment had had the bottle broken in the presence of the sepoys and severely reprimanded the surgeon, but a few days later the surgeon's bungalow was mysteriously burned down and he only just escaped with his life.

The 34th was disbanded on 6 May and the men headed for home, which, in many cases, was Oudh – already boiling with discontent after Dalhousie's annexation. Their arrival there coincided with the arrival of Sir Henry Lawrence to take up his post as Resident and, aware of the incidents in the 48th and other regiments, it didn't take him long to realise that the men of the 34th were capable of contaminating every soldier with whom they came in contact. Determined action seemed to be needed.

At this critical time, however, with the Bengal army simmering with revolt, there was no one in command. As was usual in the hot weather, but with great lack of foresight under the circumstances, General Anson and the whole of his headquarters staff had taken themselves off to the cooler hill station at Simla, from which each spring they toured the northern provinces. With the British troops, officers on leave, and their wives – all equally convinced that the storm had blown over – following in long trains of waggons, donkey carts and carriages, the whole military area of the Bengal command was virtually without central direction. The civil government was a thousand miles away in Calcutta and command was left to the seven Divisional Commanders. But as seniority in the Victorian army was virtually Holy Writ, without exception they were old men – Major-General William Hewitt, of the Meerut Division, was almost seventy – and they were almost all unfit for active service. Some had had experience of military action in recent years but on the whole they were slothful and slow and even General Anson had seen no fighting since Waterloo over forty years before.

The situation was ripe for trouble. A few officers and administrators were aware of being surrounded by an ugly atmosphere of menace but, selfish, indolent and concerned for the health of themselves and their families, on the whole the British regimental officers continued to make for the hills. The British troops, already spread thinly across India, had been thinned out even more with the recent conquest of the Punjab whose common frontier with the trouble spot of Afghanistan had drawn troops from Bengal. Most of them were now north of Meerut and Ambala. At Calcutta, there was one infantry battalion, the next was four hundred miles away at Dinapur, and there were others at Agra and Lucknow, so that in an area half as large as Europe there were only four battalions and a few reliable batteries of artillery. It wasn't hard for the troublemakers to see that their opportunity had come, and it was the British who were to start the ball rolling.

On 23 April, at Meerut, 48 miles north-east of Delhi, the commanding officer of the 3rd Light Cavalry, Colonel George Carmichael Smyth, aware of the trouble over the cartridges, ordered a parade of the regimental skirmishers, 85 picked men, the élite of the regiment and, determined to bring the matter to a head, demanded

of them, one after the other, if they would accept the cartridges. It was a stupid thing to do because his officers were well aware of the men's discontent and suspected it might be the cause of trouble. 'We may have the whole regiment in mutiny in half-an-hour if this be not attended to,' one of them had written to the adjutant, and even Hewitt, the Divisional Commander, was aware that they would have to tread carefully. But Smyth, an opinionated man, had persisted, and one after the other the men refused, only five of them agreeing. According to one young officer who watched, it was Smyth's unpopularity as much as anything else that had brought about the result.

How the 3rd Light Cavalry were disarmed and fettered.

When Smyth made his report to Hewitt, he had no option but to set up a court of inquiry, and when the findings were passed on to Anson, he did the only thing he could do and insisted that all 85 men be court-martialled for mutiny.

A court of fifteen Indian officers of both Muslim and Hindu faith was assembled. To the British it seemed the only fair method of trial but to the Indian troops the court was regarded – not without reason – as merely the mouthpiece of the Commander-in-Chief. On 8 May the sullen men were found guilty. Despite the medals many of them wore and the fact that a sentence of 'guilty' would deprive them of their pensions, none of them had attempted

29

to ask questions. The following day, owing to a stupid decision by General Hewitt that the men's shame should be seen by all, they were put into irons.

In a hollow square under a sunless sky darkened by rolling clouds, with the brass helmets of watching artillery officers catching the light with the horsehair plumes of heavy dragoons and the olive green of riflemen, the sentences were read out. Behind the unarmed Indian regiments were British troops with loaded rifles. The atmosphere was tense, the British grim-faced, the Indians indignant. The sentences stretched between five and ten years' hard labour on the roads, and as the fetters were fixed and the buttons they had worn so proudly were torn from their uniforms in a degrading scene, many of the sentenced men had tears streaming down their faces. Others shied at Smyth the boots they had taken off for the fixing of the fetters and called on their comrades to come to their help.

The fettering was a slow and clumsy business in the growing heat of the summer morning and nerves were taut as the prisoners shuffled off, some of them crying for mercy, some yelling defiantly 'For the faith! For the faith!' Shocked by their grief, General Sir Hugh Gough, then a young officer in the regiment, in an attempt to console them, visited them in the ward of the hospital where they were temporarily imprisoned. They begged him to help but he could do nothing, and that night, a Saturday and a night of leisure, he was approached by a native officer of his own troop with the information that he had business to attend to. The 'business' turned out to be a whispered warning that swords were being sharpened and that mutiny was being planned for the next day. Alarmed, Gough immediately passed on the information to his commanding officer who met it only with contempt and reproved him for listening to idle gossip. Determined to make someone listen, he went to Colonel Archdale Wilson, an artillery officer commanding the station with the local rank of brigadier. A tall, indecisive man with a fashionable tuft of beard beneath a wide, weak mouth, Wilson dodged the responsibility by saying that General Hewitt was entirely satisfied, and Gough, worried and uncertain, was left to make his way back to his bungalow through the hot, cricket-loud night.

The trouble came to a head in the evening of the next day, Sunday. The British were glad to take advantage of the day of rest because, with the grass brown and parched and the earth cracked by the sun, it was already hot enough to reduce starched linen to a limp rag. Most people were happy to do no more than join tea parties, write letters or take to their beds with the shutters closed.

As the kitehawks wheeled in the burnished sky, the British cantonments were still in the shimmering afternoon heat, and bearers and
servants dozed in the shade of verandahs. As the day cooled, the
British, their carriages and gigs raising plumes from the brown bak-
ing dust of the roads, began to prepare for the church parade and
evening service at the Church of St John's or for the usual Sunday
evening ritual of listening to the band. As he dressed, the Rev John
Rotton, gazing down the wide dusty road at the sprinkling of
distant figures in dress uniforms backgrounded by the mango
groves, palm trees and sugar cane, was warned by an Indian
woman-servant not to go. She would not be precise and, unable to
understand what she was getting at, it worried him a great deal.

British officers, women
and children listening to
the band of a native
regiment.

   The warning was not given without good reason, however, because in the dark, narrow streets of the native bazaar, heavy with
the smell of drains and the odours of little shops, the restless troopers
– or sowars – of the 3rd Light Cavalry were still indignantly de-
bating the degradation of their comrades. Nevertheless, despite the
warning Gough had received, they were still peaceable and were
only considering ways of forcing a re-trial. But wild rumours were 31

The outbreak of the
Mutiny in Meerut.

about and, goaded by the jeers of prostitutes and civilians that they
had refused to help their comrades, they were ripe for trouble and it
needed only the smallest alarm to start them to fury. It was not
long in coming.

As the 60th (Queen's) Foot fell in for the church parade, their
intentions were mistaken and word was brought by an excited
cook-boy to the Indian soldiers that they were all to be put in irons
and that the 60th were assembling to attack them. On little more
than an impulse, the cavalrymen grabbed carbines and swords and
mounted and rode for the gaol, accompanied by farriers and black-
smiths to knock off the fetters of their comrades. Even now, with
quick action, the mutiny might have been suppressed, but the
British had only recently awakened from their afternoon sleep and
there was no one about to take any positive steps.

When the excited cavalrymen charged up to the improvised gaol,
the 20th Native Infantry, which had furnished the guard, made no
resistance and the 85 mutineers were swept to freedom. By 7 pm,
hundreds of civilian prisoners, many of them riff-raff and cut-
throats eager to settle old scores, had also been set free. Together
with the soldiers and groups of agitators grasping iron-bound clubs,
who had mysteriously begun to arrive in the town from the minute
of the shackling parade, these men formed a mob and the intent
now changed from that of freeing the mutineers to murder.

32   While British soldiers were hurried to safety by friendly sepoys,

the men of the 20th and 11th Native Infantry broke into the bells-at-arms – small stone buildings behind the companies' lines, where arms were stacked after parades. The 11th were still uncertain but as their commanding officer, Colonel John Finnis, appeared in an attempt to check them he was fired on by men of the 20th and fell riddled with bullets. His death was the real start of wholesale mutiny, and Hindu and Muslim, high-caste sepoy and low-caste sapper, immediately forgot their religious differences in a common hatred of the British; muskets snapped above the yells, and smoke began to curl into the air as thatches were fired.

It was a strange fact that, while at one end of the cantonments murder was being committed, at the other sepoys were still saluting their officers unaware of anything untoward happening, and while the British near the bandstand were being cut down and their children butchered, Mrs Dunbar Muter, wife of a captain in the 60th, was waiting outside the church in her carriage for the regiment to turn up. When she was warned that, due to 'an outbreak', there would be no service, Mrs Muter had the same placid confidence of all the British. 'A slight disturbance would not stop the service,' she said, and decided to wait. Half an hour later, however, when nothing had happened, she had the horses' heads turned towards home and instantly saw that the native troops' lines were on fire and that the horizon was blood-red as if the whole cantonment were in flames. As she hurried home, she saw two European artillerymen being pursued by a throng of Indians who were hurling at them everything they could lay their hands on.

As the noise increased, alarmed officers mounted and rode out to find out what had happened and, seeing their men approaching them, rode towards them quite confidently, certain that they could mean no harm. The next second they found themselves fighting for their lives. While frantic bleeding men ran to give the alarm, military buildings and European bungalows burst into flames, and Hugh Gough, riding to the cavalry lines, saw hundreds of sepoys dancing and yelling and blazing away in all directions. Lieutenant Mackenzie, of the 3rd, rushing as he thought to prevent his men taking vengeance on soldiers jeering at the disgrace of their regiment, was met by a British sergeant fleeing through the dusk. 'Oh, God, sir', he panted, 'the troopers are coming to cut us up!'

Certain of his authority, Mackenzie called on the pursuing troopers to halt but, like so many more, within a moment he found himself parrying the slashes of their blades. Managing to escape, he joined two other officers in an attempt to lead a charge of loyal troopers, but telegraph wires had been cut and a hanging loop 33

Indian gauntlet sword.

lifted him from the saddle, so that the whole horde of horsemen poured over him. Unhurt, he remounted and rejoined his men but by now the mutineers were sweeping down on the carriages and gharries of unsuspecting Europeans, slashing at the occupants, some of the civil police joining in with their heavy staves to dismount white men as they appeared demanding help. Since officers who had influence over their men were all too often the first victims, it was clear that, although the outbreak had been spontaneous, it had been directed by men of ruthlessness and intelligence, who aimed at silencing first their most dangerous opponents.

The swift darkness saved some as they hurried along roads packed thick with excited Indians waving sticks and torches, their figures black against the flames, but Lieutenant Mackenzie, trying by this time to find his sister and her woman friend, saw a palanquin-gharry rushing towards him driverless, alongside it a trooper of his own regiment leaning in through the open window as he rode, to drive his sword again and again into the dead body of a white woman. He was cut down at once by Lieutenants Craigie and Clarke.

As the town was given up to loot and murder, both men and women struggled through the confusion to reach the safety of their homes, driving through howling crowds whose faces were contorted with fury in the light of the flames. All too often they failed and all too often it would have been of little use if they had succeeded. As the mob swept through the bungalows, fleeing screaming white women were hacked down by the long, curved cavalry tulwars or beaten to death by iron-bound cudgels, their half-naked bodies left sprawled and bleeding among the shrubs and flowers of their own gardens. The pregnant wife of the adjutant of the 3rd was caught in her home and butchered by a slaughterer from the market, while another officer's wife saw her husband shot dead before her eyes and then, because they had had smallpox and the mutineers were afraid of the infection, died in agony as they threw burning brands at her and set her clothes alight. Sometimes servants they had believed loyal helped to kill them, but there were also other instances where servants, friendly sepoys and tradesmen showed the greatest devotion and sheltered them at enormous danger to themselves.

The outbreak had clearly been unplanned because the men were later found to have made no provision for their families. Had they thought about it, they might never have risen, because there were almost as many British troops of all arms available in Meerut as there were Indian, together with twelve field guns. When they

Lieutenant Watson
(later General) of the
1st Punjab Cavalry
winning the V.C. in
November 1857.

Top The Nana Sahib, ruler of Cawnpore where the British were massacred in 1857.

Left and right centre Kin Singh, a Rajput nobleman, and Lakhsmi Bai, Rani of Jhansi, who both opposed the British in the 1858 campaign in Central India.

Bottom Baiza Bai, Queen of Sindhia, ruler of Gwalior, an ally of the British.

realised what had occurred they were probably appalled because
what they had done ought to have brought immediate bloody
reprisals. But the British were totally unprepared and nothing was
done in the chaos.

Colonel Smyth, as Duty Field Officer, decided to leave his
juniors to handle the outbreak he had caused and rode through the
blazing streets, pistol in hand, to inform the Civil Commissioner,
the General, and Brigadier Wilson. General Hewitt, though noted
as a whist player, was considered 'not a very brilliant man' and had
been posted to Meerut from Peshawar because he was 'too inactive'. He was so obese, in fact, he could no longer ride and had to
have a specially-made carriage for inspecting his troops. His
reaction to Smyth's news was to cry 'Oh, why did you have a
parade? If you had only waited another month or so, all would have
blown over,' while Archdale Wilson, not a man of action at the best
of times, was just recovering from smallpox. While Wilson and
Hewitt hedged, according to Mrs Muter it was the older rank and
file who took the first concerted action.

Time-serving soldiers, on the whole they had no knowledge of the
Indians and had no wish to have any. Living in indifferent conditions, assailed always by smallpox, cholera and dysentery, only a   37

few of them had married native wives. Their chief relaxation was drink but discipline was good and, now, the convalescent, the excused, those going on pass, all rushed to the ranks.

Unfortunately, an officious sergeant-major, rigid in the habits of the service, instead of bringing them into action at once, sent them back to change into service uniform and call the roll, while the 6th Dragoon Guards, or Carabiniers – also turned out promptly by their colonel and awaiting orders – were sent by mistake not to the parade grounds of the mutinous regiments where they might have been of some value, but to a gaol some distance away so that they were unavailable. The night was well set in before Wilson, collecting the 6oth Rifles, artillery and officers from mutinied regiments, reached the sepoys' parade grounds, where they were joined by the returning Carabiniers.

By this time, however, there were no sepoys in sight and, believing them to be about to attack the European quarters, the men were led there and a volley of bullets was sent harmlessly into the flames. It served no more purpose than to kill a few looters among the mangoes, because the mutineers, with the released men in small groups among them, many still wearing their fetters, were by this time heading out of town through the white powdery dust towards Delhi. For every active mutineer among them there were probably nine others who, finding themselves involved by the actions of the few, felt themselves compromised. As one of them said, 'There is one knave and nine fools.'

They were unorganised and had no artillery and, fully aware of the enormity of what they had done, were terrified of what would happen to them. But there was no one following. General Hewitt and Brigadier Wilson never even thought of pursuit. An officer of the Carabiniers, Captain Charles Rosser, offered to chase the fleeing mutineers with two squadrons and a few guns, with men of the 60th riding on limbers and spare waggons; while Lieutenant Möller, of the 11th, because the telegraph had been tampered with, asked to be allowed to ride with a warning to Delhi. Their offers were refused. Wilson could not believe that the mutineers would head for a place where there was a whole steady brigade which could be used against them, and was well aware that many of the British troops at his disposal were only recruits and that many of the artillerymen did not know how to handle a carbine, while the Carabiniers, for all their promptness, had only just arrived from England and, in many cases, were still unable to handle their horses. Forgetting that the station was now freed of its dangerous elements and he could have protected it with half the men at hand, he worried only about Meerut.

Terrified like Wilson of the inexperienced British soldiers being ambushed on the dark night-time roads, Hewitt made no attempt to countermand his orders and the British were led hopelessly away to bivouac on the racecourse, not even attempting to help the suffering people they were there to protect. Only a few like Lieutenant Möller made any attempt to bring anyone to justice and his single-handed arrest of the murderer of a brother-officer's wife showed what could have been done if someone had tried. But no such attempt was made by Wilson or Hewitt and, because of their inactivity, the villagers around came to believe, until a few of Rosser's dragoons appeared on the 24th, that not a single Englishman had been left alive in Meerut.

It was all over in a matter of two hours and by next day the city was silent and deserted and the men of the mutinous regiments were allowed to stream away to form the nucleus of a greater and much more serious uprising which was seized on at once by the discontented princes.

Chapter 3

Murder
at Delhi

Delhi was of the utmost importance to the British. Lying as it did across the route to the new possessions in the Punjab, insurrection there would cut the British army in two. In addition, its capture by mutineers would mean the loss of a vast arsenal of heavy guns, thousands of stands of arms and barrels of powder. What was more important, however, was that for three hundred years Delhi had been the capital of the Moghuls, the rulers of the Muslim Empire in India, and though old and ill, and reduced by the British to virtual bondage, the last Moghul king still lived there.

Whoever commanded this walled city could command the respect of all India. 'Men from all parts of Asia meet in Delhi,' Napier had said, 'and some day or other much mischief will be hatched within those walls.' Now the mutineers from Meerut, cheered on by villagers and surrounding the original 85 men who had provoked the spark that had set the countryside alight, were advancing on it, singing and shouting, aware that they had easily outmanoeuvred their British masters. They had been lucky, however. Had Hearsey or Sir Sidney Cotton, of Peshawar, been in command, they would have chanced an ambush in the urgency of the moment and few of the mutineers would ever have reached Delhi. However, covering the forty-odd miles from Meerut during the night, the first of them arrived early on 11 May, a long straggling procession of horsemen in French-grey jackets, surrounded by a cloud of yellow dust.

The road into Delhi crossed the River Jumna – at this point almost a mile wide – by a bridge of lighters lashed together and covered with logs, which was under the domination of the Red Fort, the king's personal palace, and in sight of his private quarters. Unfortunately Mohammed Bahadur Shah, the last descendant of the Moghul conquerors, had long since ceased to hope that he might throw off British domination. Eighty-two years old and an effeminate poetaster brought up in the vicious atmosphere of a decadent court, he existed on a stipend of £120,000 a year from the East India Company, still surrounded by a shabby retinue, a tiny, ailing man, none too clean, wandering-eyed and toothless. Too old to care what happened, his home was within the dusty blood-red enclosure of the fort, where filth lay side by side with rich carpets, and ivory and silver chairs were covered by dirty rags. About him there were enclosed courtyards, mysterious alleyways, secret doors and crumbling walls where elderly pensioners lived and young men and women without occupation took to debauchery

Opposite
British families slaughtered in the courtyard of the Red Fort.

41

The Bridge of boats over
the Jumna, across which
the Meerut rebels
arrived.

and intrigue for amusement. Incest, poisonings and torture were commonplace; wives intrigued against each other and mothers against sons; and court officials scoured the country for beautiful girls to sell as slaves to officials and princelings within the palace.

Among the men surrounding the king were those who longed to turn the tables on the nation which had usurped Moghul power, and they saw at once that the king was an obvious rallying point for the disaffected soldiery. In this they were quite right, and again and again as the mutiny spread, the first act of the mutineers was always to declare for him and their first cry wherever they were was 'To Delhi!' It was not the result of a discussion but a spontaneous reaction, and even rebel leaders did not hesitate to declare themselves subservient. Aware of this possibility, the British should have been well prepared, and indeed, many Europeans in Delhi had asked that the old man be removed before he could gain too much power. It was well known that, in the centre of the intriguers, his youngest wife was plotting to overcome the Company's directive that, although his son would inherit everything on his death, he could never be king and would have to leave Delhi.

Incredibly enough, despite Hewitt and Wilson, a warning of the early events at Meerut had actually arrived the previous evening, just before the telegraph line had been cut. But when it reached his

home the Commissioner, Simon Fraser, was asleep and his servant did not like to wake him and he did not receive the message until that morning, not very long before the mutineers began to stream across the bridge of boats, cheering wildly at the frail old figure who appeared in alarm on the balcony to watch. As he at last realised what was happening, Fraser hurried off to give warning to the British officers commanding the Company's troops in their cantonments on the Ridge, a rocky spine of land two miles to the north-west of the city. He was already too late, however, and events were even now far ahead of the British.

The sepoys at Delhi had long since shown their disapproval of sentences imposed on men who had refused the greased cartridges, and there had recently been rumours that Russia, always posing a threat to British India and reputedly seeking vengeance for her defeat in the Crimea, would come to their aid and re-establish the Moghul Empire. There was no attempt to stop the mutinous 3rd Light Cavalry as they swarmed over the river and up to the palace, accompanied by the king's bodyguard firing their weapons in a noisy salute. Almost at once they were joined by hordes of red-coated infantrymen in their bell-shaped shakoes who had now also begun to arrive.

Unfortunately for them, Bahadur Shah was hardly fitted to serve

Left A rebel trooper.

Right Mutinous artilleryman.

43

even as a symbol. Had the rebels been given a better rallying point, there seems little doubt that there would never have been a future for the British in India, but the king was as terrified of the mutineers as he was of the British and, seeing what was happening, Captain Charles Douglas, commander of the ceremonial force of artillery and infantry attached to his bodyguard, tried to close the gates of the city on the river side, sure that loyal forces had been summoned from Meerut and would soon arrive. In fact, of course the telegraph wires were cut and General Hewitt and Brigadier Wilson were still barricading themselves behind a fortified entrenchment against rebels who had long since fled.

Rumours of trouble had been about for some time and now, seeing the mutinous men of Meerut pouring into the city, terrified women and children began to arrive at the Kashmir Gate – the nearest exit from the city to the British camp – where, as it happened, the guard was furnished by the 38th, that regiment which had already acquired a record of successful disobedience when it had refused in 1852 to cross the 'Black Water' to Burma and got away with it unpunished. Those who had carriages and gigs and ponies began to toil up the dusty road to the Ridge in the hot summer wind, towards what they thought was safety and, on the instructions of Brigadier Harry Graves, the senior British officer, began to assemble at the Flagstaff Tower, a four-storey building 150-feet-high overlooking the city, where the Union Jack flew.

Learning from Fraser what was happening, Graves immediately ordered away the 54th Native Infantry, under Colonel John Ripley. They met the mutineers at the Kashmir Gate but, as they came face to face, the 54th, allowing the mutineers to approach without attempting to fire, turned on their own officers and most of them were shot or bayoneted to death. It settled the fate of the city.

Those civilians who had been slow to move were trapped, and both male and female became the victims of the mob from the fly-noisy bazaars in the same orgy of bloodshed, looting and wrecking that had been witnessed at Meerut. Douglas was among the first to die. Injured in an attempt to escape, he was trapped in his quarters with the Rev. Midgly Jennings, a Delhi missionary who had been visiting him with his daughter, Annie, and her friend, Mary Clifford. Fraser and John Ross Hutchinson, the Collector, had already been caught on the stairs and hacked to death and Fraser's head was being carried through the streets on the end of a sword as the mob burst down the door and murdered Douglas and Midgly and the two girls, who were dragged screaming from

a wardrobe where they had hidden.

Even as they fell, other British officials, their wives, sons and daughters, were being cut down as the end of all British authority in the city came in a welter of blood. Those who lived and worked in the area of offices, schools and courthouses were the first to die. The staff of *The Delhi Gazette* were battered to death even as they prepared an extra edition with the news of the mutiny, while other rebels stormed through churches and courthouses, hacking at the fittings and anyone who happened to be in their way. The bank manager and his wife were murdered as they defended themselves on the roof with shotgun and hog spear, then the mob poured through the narrow streets to seek out the residents of Daryaganj, a suburb at the other side of the city occupied by minor European officials and Eurasian families. As the mob swept down on them, these too were butchered except for forty-odd who were thrown into a room beneath the palace, only to be dragged out later and

The Flagstaff Tower on the Ridge at Delhi where British families gathered on the outbreak there.

45

slaughtered like cattle in a courtyard of the Red Fort – with the
exception of one woman, Mrs Aldwell, who saved the lives of herself and her children by becoming a Muslim. Those who had had
the luck to get to the Kashmir Gate spent the rest of the day there,
terrified, yet no attempt was made even now to get them away to
the cantonment.

As the news of the butchery in the city reached the Ridge, the
women crowded in the Flagstaff Tower with their children
wondered what was to happen next. The heat was appalling and
the tower was not designed for large numbers. Many of the women
were in a fainting condition and many were already mourning
murdered husbands, sons or brothers. The position looked hopeless.
With the twelve hours' grace that had been granted to them by the
supineness of Hewitt and Wilson, the Meerut mutineers were now
securely establishing themselves in the city and the fort. But while
the soldiers hesitated, two young Eurasian signallers, William
Brendish and J. W. Pilkington, in their cabin between the Ridge
and the city walls, sensing that the Postmaster, Charles Todd, had
been murdered while out seeking the fault in the line to Meerut,
had the sense to send a signal to the Commander-in-Chief at Simla.
46   Already aware of trouble at Meerut, they had heard that the

mutineers had arrived in Delhi and that the 54th had killed their
colonel, and as wounded, bleeding and exhausted soldiers stumbled
from the city past their cabin towards the Ridge they tapped out a
warning: 'We must leave office. All the bungalows are being burnt
down by the sepoys from Meerut. We are off. Mr Todd . . . is dead
I think. . . . We learn that nine Europeans were killed.' Then they
closed down their cabin and, with Mrs Todd and her child who
had taken refuge with them, fled themselves.

The Red Fort, Delhi.

It was said later that the telegraph saved India and certainly, as
the message was passed on from station to station, alert officers
prepared for trouble. At Lucknow, Sir Henry Lawrence, who only
a few days before had appealed to the Governor-General, Canning,
for sympathetic treatment of the Indians and Indian soldiers before
it was too late and they were all swept away, said, 'It will mean the
rising of the whole army throughout the country.' Other people,
both men and women, as they heard what had happened, began to
remember the signs of approaching trouble they had all seen but
had been too blind to notice – the canniness of Indian traders over
cheques and the inexplicable behaviour of old servants who had
burst into tears in the past months and begged them to go on leave to
the hills.

Back on the Ridge, with the breathless Indian heat heavy over everything, Brigadier Graves had by this time sent messengers by road for help. But they had not got through and, unaware that the supine Hewitt had done nothing, he continued to remain in expectation of reinforcements. By the afternoon, those who had escaped had begun to eye the Indian troops with them with grave doubts, uncertain whether to trust them or not. No one knew what had happened to their friends in the city and they were all aware by now that the main magazine, the arsenal of all the northern army, three miles outside, had been taken over by the mutineers. By an incredible folly, not even a company of British soldiers had been placed on it as guard and the native guard had not hesitated to join the mutineers. Now, another smaller magazine, six hundred yards from the Kashmir Gate, was blown sky-high by a group of British under Lieutenant Willoughby who had barricaded themselves inside, carrying with it hundreds of mutineers who were trying to break in. Miraculously, several of the British survived, blackened, singed, their uniforms almost blasted off their bodies. The explosion shook the earth and as the vast column of smoke and red dust rose into the bright brassy sky it was the signal to all those still at the Kashmir Gate that the end had come.

Confusion already reigned there and now the muskets of the 38th were turned on the crowd of officers and civilians. Men fell and women screamed as horses reared; it was obviously a case of every man for himself. Lieutenant Edward Vibart, a nineteen-year-old survivor of Ripley's 54th, who had run to the gate after the butchery of his comrades, realised with horrible clarity that if he stayed where he was he would be murdered, and he fled up the ramp that led from the courtyard of the gate to the bastion above. Both men and women followed Vibart's example as the bullets flattened themselves against the stonework. The only exit was over the walls and, fastening their sword-belts together, the officers used them as a rope to the ditch 25 feet below, and while some of them stayed on the bastion others went down to catch the terrified women as they fell. Climbing out of the ditch was a fearful task under the crackling of muskets as the sepoys on the wall potted at them. Again and again, as the earth crumbled under their clutching hands, they rolled back, but at last, dirty and covered with blood, they disappeared under a hail of bullets into the countryside where they were found five days later by a scouting party from Meerut under Gough and Mackenzie.

As they fled, in that area below the Ridge where many of the British had lived, the last Europeans were being sought out by the

The Kashmir Gate,
with the wall and ditch
which officers and their
wives had to cross.

mob in a deadly game of hide-and-seek. Escaping often in night
clothes or underclothes, they hid in the undergrowth and among
crumbling walls, women who had never had to lift a finger until
that day showing extraordinary resource. Some loaded their
families into carriages and literally smashed their way through the
mob to military outstations. Others hid in drains or ruins, or threw
themselves – sometimes in vain – on the mercy of Indian servants or
acquaintances.

As the magazine had exploded, the sepoys on the Ridge had
almost to a man snatched up their arms and rushed into the city.
Without them, the British were well aware that they could now
never stay where they were. The deserted bungalows were already
ablaze and the owners had to look on and watch their possessions
go up in flames, then, left only with the clothes they wore, they set
off in the growing dusk for Ambala or Kurnal, devoid of food or
money, some of them in carriages, some on stumbling exhausted
horses, some on foot. Once again no attempt at organisation or
escort was made and they arrived worn out, their shoes falling from
their feet, desperately hungry and plagued by the heat, sick at heart
and wondering just what had happened to the secure leisured
world they had known.

Chapter 4

The Fort of Despair

The news of the outbreak was received in various ways. Lord Canning heard of it almost by accident – by means of a private telegram from the Postmaster at Meerut to his aunt in Agra advising her not to go to Meerut for an intended visit because of a rising of the cavalry there. At Ferozepur, Captain Charles Griffiths, of the 61st (Queen's) Foot, was making ice cream when his major burst in and sank breathless into a chair with the news, 'All the Europeans in India have been murdered!' The Hon Julia Inglis, wife of the colonel of the 32nd (Queen's) Foot at Lucknow, was out driving with her husband when the chaplain galloped up with a message from Sir Henry Lawrence. To Harriet Tytler, wife of a British officer at Delhi, the news had been brought by a tailor who had burst in, terrified and shouting to her husband, 'Sahib, sahib, the army has come!', while at Agra, John Colvin, the Lieutenant-Governor, announced to his men with true Victorian deference to the Almighty and His servants, 'Those rascals at Delhi have killed a clergyman's daughter and if you have to meet them in the field you will not forget this.'

The information did not reach the Commander-in-Chief until late the following day. It arrived in Lahore early on Tuesday morning and, although the Chief Commissioner for the Punjab, Sir John Lawrence, brother of Sir Henry Lawrence, was away in Rawalpindi, his deputy, Robert Montgomery, acted with speed and decision. The message was passed on at once via Ambala, where General Sir Henry Barnard, the Divisional Commander, had his headquarters, and he immediately sent his son galloping on to Simla in the heat of the afternoon to inform Anson.

Anson was a great authority on whist and horses and a notable member of London society – indeed, his decision to go to India had surprised his fashionable friends because it was never the habit of well-heeled officers to accept posts outside England. He was at dinner when the message was handed to him and, not wishing to interrupt the meal, he placed it under his plate.

When he opened it after the women had left the room, he was horrified. A thousand miles of territory filled with mutinous troops lay between him and the seat of government and he had no means of reaching Canning in person. In Ambala, there was horse artillery, a British regiment of lancers and a British regiment of foot, and the 1st and 2nd Bengal Fusiliers, as well as the 9th Light Cavalry, the 4th Irregular Cavalry and the 5th and the 60th Bengal Infantry; but, although he had troops at hand, his only arsenal was now in the hands of the mutineers at Delhi. And, with the peace-

Opposite
To look after 10,000 soldiers there would have to be 30,000 camp followers.

51

time economy measures in force, the army transport organisation had fallen into disuse since the Sikh Wars eight years before and to move an army it was now necessary to rely on civilian contractors. The system had recommended itself to one government after another because it was cheap but unhappily it was also almost unworkable because, since there were hardly any railways, carts for the baggage had to be painstakingly rounded up – much to the annoyance of the native owners who were quick to dismantle or hide them rather than let them go – together with the bullocks to draw them, elephants for the heavy guns and camels for the baggage. As the cavalry were normally used in this work, Anson was doubly impeded because most of them had already gone over – either in fact or in spirit – to the mutineers. In addition the army had need of enormous numbers of the camp followers – the grooms, the water carriers, the grass-cutters, the syces, the sweepers, and the servants – who made the moving of an army in India such a vast undertaking. At times, to look after 10,000 soldiers there would have to be 30,000 followers and the whole force would occupy miles of countryside, creating a vast moving dust cloud and swallowing up provisions and forage as it advanced. To complicate matters further, Anson had no ammunition, no medical stores, no hospitals, no litters for the wounded, no drugs, not even any bandages. It would need days to requisition what he wanted and, in the meantime, some regiments had no more than 20 rounds of ammunition per man, and there were no guns heavy enough to breach the 12-foot-thick walls of Delhi.

Nevertheless, he alerted his command and got the Bengal Fusiliers moving within two days. By 17 May, thanks to the driving energy of a few individuals, 500 carts, 2,000 camels, 2,000 coolies and over 2 million pounds of grain had been acquired and an army, known as the Delhi Field Force, had been raised, while Sir John Lawrence, on his own authority, had written to London demanding infantry reinforcements. Lawrence, one of the titans of British India, was a 'vehement, swift-riding man', – 'an old bullock', as he said himself, for work. Hard-headed and realistic and more able than his brother, Henry, in the eyes of one of his detractors he was 'a rough, coarse man, in appearance more like a navvy than a gentleman'. But he was not blinded by sentiment or emotion and he was also an intensely active man and had been badgering Anson from the first moment of alarm, refusing to accept his wish for time to 'collect his resources' or the Commissariat's requirements of 16 to 20 days to procure provisions. But Anson knew his job, too, and would not allow himself to be hurried by an impatient civilian with

no knowledge of his difficulties. He knew only too well what lay ahead. By this time Canning had wired warning him that the country between Delhi and Cawnpore was passing into the hands of the rebels and, firmly believing that Delhi could be disposed of with artillery, asking him to prevent it. But Canning had only partly grasped the situation. He had realised the danger but his military advisers in Calcutta were soldiers in name only and neither they nor he had any idea of the difficulties which had to be overcome before Anson could march. Cawnpore and Delhi were 266 miles apart and he had only 2,900 men.

However, he had started things moving and a peremptory message had gone to Meerut demanding action. It had been carried by William Stephen Raikes Hodson, whom Anson had instructed to set up an espionage system. Hot-headed, volatile and careless with money, Hodson enjoyed war. A man of medium height, yellow-haired with bright blue eyes, he had a frank challenging manner but he was unorthodox and had been removed from command of the Corps of Guides for being in trouble over money. Nevertheless he was to prove to be one of the great personalities thrown up by the Mutiny, and, despite a broken ankle, he rode the 150-odd miles from Kurnal with nothing but a small escort of Sikh horsemen and was back in Ambala in four days.

A view of Wheeler's entrenchment from the rebel lines, showing the battered barrack blocks and the unfinished buildings from which the mutineers sniped.

53

The Bengal Fusiliers
were on the march to
the relief of Delhi
within two days.

Now, while one column under Archdale Wilson finally set off
from Meerut, in close hot weather with not a breath of wind in the
air and the sun like a ball of fire, another under Anson set off from
the north. Villages suspected of ill-using the refugees from Delhi
were burned en route and the men hanged. On the 27th, Anson
died of that scourge of all Victorian armies, cholera – though the
unkind considered it was 'an attack of John Lawrence' that had
killed him.

Connected by telegraph to Calcutta only through Karachi, the
army now found itself without even a head, and the command was
taken over by Sir Henry Barnard, a man of advanced years quite
unaccustomed to campaigning in the intense heat of India. However, he was a brave soldier who had had recent experience of war
in the Crimea and, having learned there what delay could do, he
pushed on at speed. His march was a great achievement. Heads
down, the men trudged through the sultry nights into the teeth of
the hot dry wind and the clouds of driving dust. Footsore, faces
coated with sweat, they were often asleep as they marched, the
rumble of the guns heavy behind them with the clinking of bits and
the jangling of equipment. Joining forces with Wilson who, stirred
at last out of his torpor, had fought two small battles en route,
Barnard defeated a strong force of mutineers at Badli-ke-serai on

8 June, though not without severe loss, and the same day his men appeared among the burned-out cantonments at Delhi, where for four phantom weeks the mirage of a restored Moghul Empire had existed unmolested.

Meanwhile panic had spread to the rest of the country, even to Calcutta where Lord Canning ruled. Many of the Europeans there knew even less of the Indians than the officials up-country because their business seldom carried them beyond the city boundaries. The trouble at Barrackpore had been only a night's march away, however, and they were terrified that the occupants of the bazaars and native quarters would rise against the white population and plunder the great commercial capital. Men went to the office with loaded weapons on their knees and the ships plying to the coast were packed with their families. With rumours in the bazaar that an uprising was imminent, the traditional *feu de joie* for the Queen's birthday was fired from muskets, not the new rifles, while many Europeans stayed away from the celebratory ball for safety. Women hired sailors from the ships to protect them, only to find they were a bigger menace than the natives, while the traditional Indian wedding fireworks threw everyone into constant terror.

There was a similar and even more undignified panic in Simla where it was believed that the Gurkhas, the Nepalese hillmen who had served with the British for many years as mercenaries, had joined the rebels. Chivalry was momentarily forgotten and, though the Deputy Commissioner and regimental officers stayed at their posts, other men outdid the women in their efforts to escape, even offering bribes to bearers to carry their baggage and leave the women to shift for themselves. The women didn't hesitate to get their own back after the panic was over with a notice in the local paper to the effect that they were to hold a meeting to discuss measures 'for the protection of the gentlemen', and offering to make pillows for them 'stuffed with the purest white feathers'.

At Lahore, the capital of the Punjab, there was little trouble. Sir John Lawrence's deputy, Montgomery, had a plentiful supply of British troops, and when the telegram from Delhi arrived, the Indian regiments were promptly investigated. Discovering they were unreliable, it was decided to disarm them.

Elaborate plans had been worked out to allay the suspicion of the sepoys and the suspense was hidden behind the ceremony of a regimental ball. Throughout a hot evening men in the secret behaved as if there were nothing in their minds but enjoyment but when the sepoys marched on to the parade ground the following morning, they heard disbandment orders read aloud and were 55

Barnard's defeat of the mutineers at Badli-ke-Serai.

instructed to pile arms. As they hesitated, it dawned on them that the outnumbered British troops were lined up behind them, their rifles loaded, their muzzles pointing towards them, and that beyond them, visible through long corridors between them, were cannon loaded with case-shot, a gunner holding a portfire at each breech.

Their officers, who had continued to trust their men implicitly, stared unbelieving and even threw down their own weapons in rage, but the deed was done without bloodshed. Despite the bitter protests of their colonels, doubtful regiments were also disarmed in Peshawar, Amritsar, Multan and other places. At Ferozepur, retribution came quickly. The 57th Native Infantry had not molested their officers and had even saluted them as they had announced they were disbanding themselves, but men who were taken in arms were hanged or blown from guns. This form of execution, last used in 1825, had been the recognised punishment for mutiny and rebellion throughout India for hundreds of years and was a favourite of the Moghul emperors. It was hated by both Muslims and Hindus on religious grounds, but the men were stoical as they were led to the guns by a band playing popular airs. Only at the last moment did they break into wild imprecations at the men who were bringing them to their shameful end, then, as the guns fired, heads and limbs were seen to fly into the air, and there was a sickly, pungent smell of burned flesh. The artillerymen, neglecting to put up backboards for the guns, were spattered by an obscene shower of blood and entrails and fragments of flesh.

Such punishments were horrifying – but far from new even among the Indians – and, unfamiliar with the country and de-

56

pendent on out-of-date advisers, Canning at first worried that they were judging men guilty before they were proved so. But it had always been Lawrence's policy to back up to the hilt the actions of his junior officers, and there was no mercy. Severe as Lawrence and his officials were, they probably saved hundreds of lives, both British and Indian, because if the Punjab had gone the whole country would have risen, and by their actions the one source of British troops had been secured. They disarmed 36,000 men, confiscated 69,000 stands of arms, forbade iron-bound clubs and brought in restrictions on the sale of all chemicals concerned with the manufacture of gunpowder.

The Punjab had always been different, however. It had benefited from annexation and its tribes were virile fighters who had given the British a hard battle. Proud of their resistance, they did not resent the British half as much as they resented the despised and swaggering sepoys from Oudh whom they felt they could eat alive but who, under British leadership, had conquered them. Nevertheless, Lawrence was under no delusions and knew they were only waiting to see which way the battle would go but, with every doubtful sepoy disarmed, he could now strip the countryside of British troops and raise new moveable columns from the wild tribes of the north for the help of Delhi. Loyal princes could also offer reinforcements from Kashmir and their provinces, both to guard the Grand Trunk Road which led from the northern frontier down the valley of the Ganges to Calcutta, and for a grand attack on Delhi which, if it fell to the British, would help to keep Lucknow, Allahabad and Cawnpore safe.

57

Unfortunately, while the plan was good, it depended on strong action being taken in the places it was most likely to affect, but at Cawnpore, strategically sited across the route north, General Sir Hugh Wheeler, a slight, spare sixty-eight-year-old Irishman with fifty years of excellent service to his credit, had done all the wrong things. While officers in other districts, sticking with Victorian rigidity to the habits of the day, faced out difficult regiments, unnerving them even with their commonplace activities, Wheeler's moves, though always designed for the safety of his command, had only served to bring on trouble. The usual rumours had been heard and the Europeans and Eurasians were apprehensive of the as yet undefined danger – 'Everybody in the station,' it was said, 'seemed to think that something dreadful was to occur, but was unable to foresee what it was.' Though British troops were expected within three weeks and the native troops appeared to be quiet, 'yet something indefinite and alarming overshadowed the minds of all.'

Hearing from his spies in the city that there was to be an outbreak on 24 May, Wheeler had forbidden public celebrations – attendance at church, the pealing of bells and the normal salute of guns – for the Queen's birthday, which fell on that day. His belief was that they might spark off rebellion but, in fact, their absence had served only to unnerve the British more. Cawnpore was a lively station, situated like so many others in the days before railways on the banks of the Ganges, in a broad dusty plain. It was a straggling city with an Assembly Room and a Masonic Hall and, because it was planned to make it a railway centre, there were many European and Eurasian civilian families there. Wheeler, popular but old and uncertain, was worried by the situation. It was clear that trouble was coming. Hinted warnings had been given and the shopkeepers in the bazaars had kept their shutters up, while servants had stayed away from work either because they were afraid or because they were rebellious.

The steamers had been carrying civilian families downriver to Allahabad for some time and the tension was contagious. There were numerous small incidents and the uncertainty and indecision began to affect the nerves of the officers who felt that anything was better than the unhealthy suspense and were inclined to put the men to the test to see whether they were likely to remain loyal. 'I do not wish to write gloomily,' Colonel Ewart, of the 1st Native Infantry, wrote, 'but there is no use disguising the fact that we are in the utmost danger . . . and if the troops do mutiny, my life must almost certainly be sacrificed.'

The Nana Sahib,
Rajah of Bithur.

Despite being past an active military age, Wheeler was no Hewitt, however, and, a constant rider, he was not lacking in energy. He had seen the dangers of the greased cartridge and had been in constant touch with Henry Lawrence at Lucknow fifty miles away. But, because his wife, who was an Indian, was a close friend and caste-fellow of the Nana Sahib, the Rajah of Bithur, Wheeler considered himself safe, and lucky in the hour of crisis to have at hand a powerful Indian prince he could trust. The Nana Sahib was a Mahratta, a corpulent, lively man of thirty-six with black restless eyes and a face marked by smallpox. He lived only a few miles away and was considered to be more British than the British themselves. Though he spoke no English, he enjoyed having newspapers from England translated for him and had food sent to him from Fortnum and Mason. He associated with the officers from Meerut, attended their races, and gave parties for them, on occasion even pressing on them embarrassingly expensive gifts. He had offered two guns and six hundred men, both cavalry and infantry.

In Lucknow, Henry Lawrence was less sure of him and he was considered there by Martin Gubbins, the Financial Commissioner, to be arrogant, presuming and deceitful. On the death of his father, the dethroned peshwa or ruler of the Mahratta dynasty, his pension had not been passed on to his adopted son, the Nana Sahib, because it was argued the king had been paid enough to have made the future secure for both of them, and now, though Wheeler did not know it, the Nana Sahib was burdened with debt. Though he had inherited a fine palace, Government stock and over £200,000 59 worth of jewels, gold ornaments, silver and coinage, much of his fortune had gone on pensions for the old king's 15,000 retainers, and his expenditure now doubled his income, and he was left with nothing of his former glory but a reduced and insignificant title. A small concession – even only of title – might well have kept him loyal but there was no British official imaginative enough to sense the answer to his resentment.

Despite the warnings, however, Wheeler would hear nothing against him but, hoping to keep things quiet until the rising of the Ganges allowed steamers to arrive in Cawnpore with reinforcements, he had tried to decide on a site for a safe shelter in the event of trouble for all the British families for whom he was responsible. He had chosen not the Magazine which, with its large stocks of weapons and ammunition, might well have been held, but two large barrack buildings, one with a thatched roof, standing in the open away from the native city. The reasons for his choice were that he had been assured by his spies that if anything happened the mutineers would march at once for Delhi, and he had felt also that the Magazine would be hard for a relieving force to reach, while the barrack buildings stood close to the Allahabad road.

He had ordered a parapet and gun emplacements to be erected round the buildings but, despite the plentiful supply of water nearby, bad staff work had resulted in little being moved in, and because of the difficulty – with the Indians sullen and rebellious – of getting workmen, the earthwork was only loosely built and was not even bullet-proof. Again because Wheeler did not expect to be molested by the mutineers, it remained only four feet high and could easily be scaled by a man on a horse. Contemptuously christened 'the fort of despair' by the Nana Sahib's agent, it only served to indicate to the Indians Wheeler's distrust of them. While he and his officers tried to show their confidence in their troops by sleeping in the cantonments, all their efforts were ruined by nervous civilians hurrying to the entrenchment at every alarm.

Because Wheeler was expecting trouble, Henry Lawrence sent him 84 men of the 32nd (Queen's) Foot in carriages, and two squadrons of Irregulars under Captain Fletcher Hayes, but such were the alarms in Cawnpore and the lack of organisation, when they arrived Hayes found only a scene of 'confusion, fear and bad arrangement'. He was confident that the European population, together with a few people from Fatehgarh, about 80 miles to the north, who had been sent down for safety, were bringing trouble on themselves because they were showing the natives 'how very easily we can become frightened'.

To guard the entrenchment against roughly 3,000 possible mutineers, Wheeler had six guns, the 84 men of the 32nd, 200 unattached officers, soldiers and civilians, and 44 native bandsmen. Of this force 74 were invalids, but there were also 60 European artillerymen and Hayes' two squadrons of Irregulars. The men the Nana Sahib had sent were noticeably posted not near the defences but near the Treasury and the Magazine. There were rations for 25 days, but they consisted largely of flour and dried peas.

In Lucknow, Sir Henry Lawrence behaved with more certainty in spite of being a sick man. As he was well aware, the British in Oudh were detested. The East India Company had broken its promises when it had taken over the province from its insomniac king, and many landowners had been dispossessed. The king had been a debauched man who had brought his removal on himself without a doubt because, under his laws, powerful landowners had 'pillaged, tortured and murdered in every direction', and no road, town, village or hamlet was secure. Robbery and murder had become their diversions, but the improvements that had been brought – roads, cheap post, the telegraph system, plans for education and irrigation – were all too often found wanting when set alongside the wholesale acquisitions Dalhousie had indulged in, and the removal of the king had brought problems for Lawrence never even considered by the British. Lucknow, a maze of dark lanes, shaded gardens and dusty palaces, was full of jobless functionaries, tradesmen and pensioners of the king – even the women of the zenana – and many of them were starving, while, with three-quarters of the state forces disbanded, there were hundreds of discontented soldiers and officials, many of them with relations in the Bengal army, to mingle with the vicious characters who had gathered in the city round the decadent court.

Sir Henry Lawrence. as a young man.

Lawrence was tall and thin, vaguely mandarin in aspect with his wide slanting eyes, large head and long beard. Indifferent to dress, he had also seemed indifferent to life since the death of his wife in 1854. Courteous, gentle, passionately devoted to the humble natives, he was a born diplomat with a sound and shrewd knowledge of the Indians whom he had never regarded with the contempt of many of his colleagues, and he was well fitted by temperament for the calm front he had to show.

While he kept up a pretence of firmness, cheerfulness and conciliation, however, he was taking no chances and was sending precise and accurate reports to Canning. Reinforcements might be expected to come from Calcutta through Allahabad and Cawnpore, but unfortunately there were few available and, with Cawnpore uncertain, he was also well aware that Allahabad, despite its importance, was garrisoned entirely by native troops.

There had been a strange lull since the initial drama at Meerut and Delhi. While the whole country waited for the expected retribution, nothing happened. British officers in the outstations deliberately continued to sleep with their wives and children among their men in an attempt to calm them with a show of confidence. Never knowing which day would be their last, they played one faction against the other in the hope that they could hold on until help came. Because there was no reaction, however, the force of rebellion gathered momentum and the calm ended on 30 May at Lucknow.

Granted the local rank of brigadier-general by Canning, Henry Lawrence's first moves were sound and sensible. On 23 May, he ordered in all the British from the outstations, and began to make preparations for a siege. Trees were cut down, ditches made deeper and sharpened stakes planted round the area of the Residency building. Provisions and munitions were quietly transferred from the Machchi Bewan, a small fortress a mile outside the Residency area, and packed in cellars and outhouses, while forage was stored and treasure was buried secretly so that it would not have to be guarded.

To be near his troops, Lawrence had moved to the army cantonments at Muriaon, three miles outside the city on the north side of the river opposite the Residency, and had placed some of the few British troops at his disposal in camp between the cantonments and the city to keep the road open in the event of an outbreak. On 30 May he was still hoping there would be no trouble but reports had now come in of an expected attack, timed to start at 9 pm. Sitting at dinner in the cantonments, while the heavy scents of the hot Indian night came through the windows, he and his staff listened to the signal gun sounding the hour.

For a moment there was an expectant silence then Lawrence leaned towards Captain Thomas Wilson, the aide who had brought the reports of the attack. 'Your friends are not punctual,' he said. Almost as he spoke, they heard the rattle of musketry and the sound of running feet, and they knew he had been wrong.

Horses, kept saddled and waiting, were brought round and Lawrence and his staff went outside to await them. Through the trees they could see the flames beginning to surge upwards from the cantonments, and just then a body of sepoys of Lawrence's bodyguard appeared and swung into line to face them. The Indian officer in command saluted and asked if they should load. Captain Wilson was horrified by the suggestion because the men were known to be discontented and before morning, in fact, had mutinied. But Lawrence said 'Yes, load by all means.' Quietly, their hearts thumping, the group waited as the clatter of the muskets rang out, but the incident passed off without trouble and Lawrence rode off to join his British troops, the 32nd Foot. By this time, several officers of the native regiments had been murdered and the bungalows were an inferno, the residents of the city watching the flames from their rooftops; but a few loyal sepoys marched out and lined up alongside the 32nd. There was a brief brush with the mutineers who withdrew to the racecourse where Lawrence attacked them in the first light of the next morning but they made little attempt to withstand him and fled.

The long suspense of waiting to see which way they would turn was over and it was at last known who were friends and who were not. Sepoys who had been taken prisoner were tried by court martial and hanged, while those who escaped joined the men from Meerut at Delhi. The outbreak, quickly handled, seemed to be over but, in fact, control had been kept only in Lucknow. On 31 May, there were risings at Bareilly and Shahjahanpur, and on 3 June, mutiny broke out at Sitapur to the north and at Faizabad, where most of the British were murdered. The trouble in Lucknow, however, seemed to have been put down, but Lawrence was taking no chances and moved back into the Residency building in the city.

Though he had acted quickly and it seemed every precaution had been taken, the outlook was not good. Dinner parties and church services were still held, but no one ventured far from the Residency. The area chosen to be defended, with its green lawns and flowerbeds, rested on a small plateau within the city boundary but it was not an easy place to hold because of its extensive perimeter. Part of it was bounded by the walls of buildings and enclosures which had been made into strongpoints but, for the rest, it consisted of a ditch and a hurriedly-erected bank of earth heightened at exposed spots by sandbags loopholed for muskets. There were two entrances, the Water Gate to the north and the Baillie Guard to the east, which were defended by barricades and artillery. Other batteries were placed at commanding points.

The Residency itself, an imposing building, was not of much use. Its windows were wide and, since it could be covered by cannon from the city, the upper floors would have to be abandoned. But, 63 as a precaution, coolies were employed to demolish the crumbling palaces and mud houses of the city which crowded too closely, only the mosques and temples being spared. Lawrence's major problem still remained the same, however, because he had far too few men to defend his position, while around and in the city were 7,000 Indian soldiers and, in the narrow alleys, 500,000 aggrieved people prepared to snatch at the mutiny as a chance to rise in rebellion. Against them he had only 700 trained European soldiers on whom he could depend, and every fit man was called in for musketry drill, while officers carried arms everywhere they went as they waited for what the next few days would bring.

The events of the Mutiny constantly interacted on each other. While the trouble in Delhi prevented any help being sent to Lucknow, the outbreak in Lucknow had the effect of reducing Wheeler's already small garrison in Cawnpore. The men Lawrence had sent him had spoken confidently of more reinforcements coming soon and, since he was nearer to Allahabad from where he could expect them, Wheeler decided to send back the men of the 32nd. On 3 June, with great unselfishness but in the face of what seemed a greater danger at Lucknow, he sent a further two officers and fifty men. 'This leaves me weak,' he wrote, 'but I trust to hold my own until more Europeans arrive.' That very evening he was warned that a rising in Cawnpore was imminent.

Once more the British crowded into the fragile entrenchment. Lawrence's warnings had not budged Wheeler's faith in the Nana Sahib but he had by this time begun to regard his Indian soldiers and his defensive position with some doubt. In a letter to Lawrence he said, 'Trust in any of the native troops is out of the question . . . of course, we can offer protection to nothing with our entrenchments.' For the moment, though, the chief concern of the families crowded into the two barrack buildings was not so much fear as discomfort. Deprived of their servants, concerned for their children in the appalling heat of the Indian summer, they slept on the verandahs trying to manage on the few sticks of furniture they had been able to bring with them, aware of the drab possibilities of their stocks of food and only too conscious of the menace they faced from the city.

It was clear now that the trouble they had hoped to avoid had finally become unavoidable and they all waited in the heat and darkness, sick with suspense. The danger they had been expecting so long was not far away. On the night of 4 June, not long after

Wheeler had sent his letter to Lawrence and following days of disagreement and argument as to who should give the signal to start, the 2nd Native Cavalry and the 1st Native Infantry finally mutinied. The first indication that something was afoot came at midnight with the rumble of wheels and the squeak of heavy limbers as guns were dragged through the thick dust. Everyone heard them and those few civilian families who had resisted the temptation to move into the entrenchment snatched up their belongings, well aware now of what to expect.

The cavalry and artillery were leaving their encampments and, though they did not harm their officers, the sepoys joined the Nana Sahib's men and seized the Treasury. A few of the 53rd Native Infantry tried to defend it but Wheeler, believing them and the 56th Native Infantry to have joined the mutineers, ordered the guns in his entrenchment to fire on their lines. At the time, the sepoys were, in fact, still peaceable but by this blunder they were immediately converted to the rebel cause, though, even now, such was Wheeler's popularity with them, the native officers and some of their men still decided to join him in the entrenchment. The remaining sepoys, as had been expected, marched off without further trouble towards Delhi.

Watching the rising dust, it was now Wheeler's belief that all he had to do was wait for relief, and some of the families inside the entrenchment actually left again. But the sepoys had gone no further than Kullianpur, the first staging post on the Delhi road, and two days later they were back. Those who had left the entrenchment were hastily rounded up and brought back, to hear that Wheeler had received a message from the Nana Sahib. Unable, at this stage, apparently, to throw in his lot wholeheartedly with the mutineers, he had sent a warning that he was about to attack.

The men and women inside the entrenchment waited with thumping hearts, staring over the earth embankment with straining eyes. From time to time they caught glimpses of men in scarlet and French grey moving among the trees across the plain, and at 10 am on that day, the 6th, the bugles blared and the defenders ran for their positions. Within moments a round shot from one of the guns of the Magazine, which Wheeler had failed to destroy, dropped alongside a party of women and children outside one of the barrack buildings and the siege had begun.

By this time the garrison had been reduced to only 240 men. Hayes, who had seen such 'confusion, fear and bad arrangement,' had been murdered by his men while out in an attempt to bring order to a rebellious district. ⊱————

Chapter 5

Massacre
at the Boats

The siege of Wheeler's fortification began for the British in Cawnpore a period of hell on earth. There was hardly a corner in the entrenchment where it was safe from bullet or round shot, no privacy, no rest from the myriads of flies, and no sleep.

There was no lack of arms, the men having two, three, sometimes as many as eight rifles each, and there seemed to be plenty of food. Though the indiscriminate distribution of rations soon came to an end and the daily issue began to consist of a handful of split peas and a handful of flour, at first private soldiers were seen trudging away with bottles of champagne and preserved herrings. Every attempt was made to supplement the supply, however, and sometimes a horse was shot when the enemy cavalry came within reach and once a sacred Brahminy bull which was grazing within rifle range.

Despite the constant firing, the chief problem was the heat. By the middle of June the exposed entrenchment had become intolerable and men who had never been in the habit of going out in the sun were dying of sunstroke under a molten sky, the flesh of their faces darkening even as they died. It was not much better in the barrack blocks where the 375 women and children waited, though half a century later a huge underground room was discovered beneath one of them which would have given a cool bullet-proof shelter. It was not long before the stink from the putrefying carcasses of dead animals became appalling, and it was impossible to lay a hand on a gun while muskets went off on their own. Thirst caused intense suffering. There was only one well and it had no protective cover from sepoy sharp-shooters. Even at night the creaking of the tackle betrayed the presence of the defenders and more than one man lost his life in an attempt to ease the suffering of the children.

It was not even possible to bury the dead. The only coffin available was used for the first casualty but after that the only thing they could do with the bodies was drop them down a disused well just outside the parapet. Indian servants suffered with their masters and several women gave birth within the entrenchment, while others saw their children shot down before their eyes as, unaware of the danger, they ran from the security of the barrack blocks to play with round shot.

After twelve days of siege Wheeler sent a message to Lucknow by an Indian messenger who slipped through the rebel lines. It ended despairingly. 'Our defence has been noble and wonderful,'

Opposite
The massacre of the boats, Cawnpore.

Wheeler wrote, 'our loss heavy and cruel. We want aid, aid, aid!' It was impossible to send aid, however. Lawrence was well aware that it was his duty to harden his heart to the appeals. A sensitive, gentle man, he suffered agonies of conscience but he had enough intelligence to know that any attempt to send help to Wheeler would only imperil Lucknow and could not save Cawnpore. Even the men of the 32nd Wheeler had returned him for his own defence would have been no help because the entrenchment had never been properly fortified and was far too frail.

By 11 June, with the sun reaching its hottest, Wheeler's garrison was suffering from the non-stop fire of thirteen guns, and by the 15th there were seven complete batteries sending in a constant storm of shot and shell to flay the earth and fill the air with drifting dust clouds. In addition, not 400 yards away were seven partially-built barracks and a chapel, and from their walls and roofs, at a height of forty feet, the rebels were able to cut down the defenders with musketry fire. Individual officers and soldiers performed miracles of courage, going out again and again in attempts to spike enemy guns, but men, women and children were still caught and torn apart by cannon shot. No prisoners were taken. It was not sense to let the mutineers know of their condition and, since the first prisoner they had taken had escaped, after that they were all 'despatched without reference to headquarters'.

On the night of the 13th in a high driving wind, the thatched roof of one of the barracks was set on fire by an enemy battery and, though the sick and wounded and the screaming women and children, their hair and clothes alight, were dragged clear, 40 sick and wounded were burned to death and almost all the medical stores were destroyed in the flames and the cascades of red-hot bricks. It was the beginning of the end for the garrison.

With the blackened walls too hot to approach, there was now no shade at all for many people and crude shanties were erected with tins, cots and canvas, and holes were scratched by desperate
mothers in the rocky ground to shelter their children. While smoke-blackened soldiers of the 32nd raked the cooling ashes of the barracks for medals they had lost, the women, begrimed with dirt, their clothes in rags, their cheeks pinched and haggard as they watched their children die, struggled to remain sane. Corpses – young girls, children and soldiers alike – were laid in rows to be dragged unceremoniously away at dusk to the disused well, and in a bedlam of groans and cries and the fretful wailing of children, they lived in the sort of hell none of them had ever dreamed could exist.

Women used to luxury found their friends smashed to pulp along-

Top On the march in Central India. John Crealock, the artist, returns to his column.

Bottom Brigadier Short, Crealock's commander in 1857.

side them and, struggling to cook horse meat, attend to ghastly
wounds, or pass out ammunition to the weary soldiers, they tried
to swallow the unappetising rations and drink water tainted at
times with the life blood of the men who had drawn it. Existing in a
world of swirling red dust, hoarding what few titbits there were for
the children and the sick, the garrison continued to hold out, their
guns silent for hours at a time in an attempt to hoard ammunition.
With many of the gunners dead, volunteers were now serving the
weapons and women were offering stockings and underclothing to
make gunpowder cartridges.

General Wheeler had virtually given up command by this time.
Shocked by the death of his son, Godfrey, whose head had been torn
off by a round shot in front of his mother and sisters, the old man lay
on a mattress in tears. On 24 June, he managed to get another note
to Lawrence. . . . 'We have no instruments, no medicines, provisions for ten days at farthest . . . we have been cruelly deserted and
left to our fate. . . . Surely we are not to die like rats in a cage.'

Senior officials of the city, in the habit of luxury, found themselves
living in a nightmare of noise and flying stones, while the condition
of the wounded, filthy, bloody and covered with clouds of flies, was
so appalling the fit were glad to remain in action and keep their
distance. On 23 June, the anniversary of Plassey, the mutineers
surged forward. As their guns roared from a distance of only a few
hundred yards, the 2nd Native Cavalry and the scarlet-coated
infantry, pushing bales of cotton before them for protection, advanced on the entrenchment. The British held their fire to the last 71

moment then smashed down the charging wall of horses and men and the rebels fell back.

The Nana Sahib, now either through choice or pressure completely throwing in his lot with the mutineers, was trying to bring some order to the rebel forces. While prisoners were treated with appalling cruelty, he was really still no nearer to defeating Wheeler than at the beginning of the siege and he began to devise a scheme to bring him out of his entrenchment.

With the rains near to make the position completely untenable and with rations for only four days left, there was never any chance of success for Wheeler but, held together by spirited young officers with no intention of surrendering, the siege might still have gone on. There was no shortage of courage, despite the constant and harassing fire that smashed down the fortifications and struck bricks and plaster in showers from the barrack buildings until there was barely a foot of their surface that was not pitted by shot. Nobody was spared. In the first week, 59 of the 60 artillerymen were dead and their guns were scarred, grooved and dented. The waist-high embankment protected no one and a private was killed by the same bullet that broke both his wife's arms and wounded the child she was carrying. When a wounded officer was hit again as he limped to the first aid post, Lieutenant Mowbray Thompson, of the 56th,

72

who went to his help, was struck also and as another officer appeared, he too was wounded. Their only reinforcement was a single cavalry officer named Bolton whose men had mutinied while on district duty from Lucknow and who spurred through the rebels and leapt the barrier to join the garrison.

The agonised women, their faces gaunt with sleeplessness, strain and personal tragedy, were too numb to complain about the conditions. Unwashed, smoke-blackened like the men, they continued to pass out ammunition and look after the sick and wounded. A swift death was merciful as the severely wounded cried out aloud in the heat, confusion and discomfort. But there was no respite for anyone in the scorched, smoke-darkened barracks and more than one was reduced to madness. The whole place stank of putrefaction, saltpetre and the thick dust from the shattered buildings. 'My God, my God, when wilt Thou deliver us?' someone wrote on one of the walls across the scarred plaster.

The entrenchment had become a charnel house by this time and, with little hope left, nobody was surprised when, on the 25th, the 21st day of the siege, with food and water scarce and the route to the well still open to heavy fire, a half-caste woman prisoner carrying a child arrived from the Nana Sahib's lines offering terms.

Despite Wheeler's complaints that they had been abandoned, Lord Canning had by no means forgotten Cawnpore, and though Lawrence, his responsibility always at Lucknow, could do nothing, the Governor-General was making tremendous efforts. A moveable column was organised and the command given to Brigadier Henry Havelock.

Although he had fought in Burma, Afghanistan, Gwalior and the Punjab and had just returned from an expedition to Persia under Sir James Outram, at sixty-two Havelock had never before held an independent command. In an age when purchase meant that a man needed money to buy promotion, he had been held back all along by poverty and lack of influence and, while men of twenty-five were buying colonelcies, he did not reach even the rank of captain until the age of forty-three. A rigid Baptist, because of his belief in temperance and the Bible classes he conducted for his soldiers he had become known as 'Holy' Havelock, a stiff-faced, unbending man only five feet five inches tall, erect, high-browed, with white hair and piercing eyes, 'as sour,' it was said, 'as if he had swallowed a pint of vinegar.'

Havelock was an unpopular man, not easy, with his stiff-necked personal discipline, for the self-indulgent Anglo-Indian society to understand. But he was eager to start, and had great faith in the help of the Almighty in this splendid opportunity which had been granted him so late in life when he had ceased to expect such chances. 'May God give me wisdom and strength,' he wrote to his wife, 'to fulfil the expectations of Government and to restore tranquillity to the disturbed districts.'

One of the things that spurred him on was the knowledge that there were women in Cawnpore and sentiment demanded that they should be saved. Unnecessary risks were to be taken again and again because women were involved and many male lives were often given for one female, when a more hard-hearted attitude would have sacrificed the one for the many. But again and again the Victorian attitude that women were fragile creatures who must be spared hardship and suffering led men to try to snatch them from danger. Havelock was no different. Though not conventionally gallant, he was a pious churchgoer who saw his duty sternly and, despite his Bible classes, could also hang men for anything he considered less than honourable.

Shrewd and capable, he knew he would have less than three thousand British troops, though others were expected to follow. It was barely sufficient, but time was of the essence, and he insisted on enough money to build up a sound intelligence service and freedom to buy as many draught and pack animals en route as he needed to keep the column moving swiftly. His object was to relieve Cawnpore, and he had great need of the prayers he said regularly, because with his insufficient forces he was proposing to fight his way through six hundred miles of hostile country in blinding sun and monsoon rain. As he was carried north on the short stretch of railway which was practically all that existed in India, he laid it down that in his column there were to be no private carriages for officers and that baggage was to be kept to a minimum in the need for speed.

By this time the whole countryside was alive with rebellion as what the Indians came to know as the Devil's Wind began to blow across the dusty plains of the sub-continent. What had begun as a military mutiny was becoming in every district where it had gone unpunished an uprising of princes and chiefs and people, with a general uprooting of every sign of authority by the wilder and less responsible spirits. Hundreds of Europeans and Eurasians were already hiding in bushes and ruins and native houses, entirely dependent on the good will of their servants or the people who had befriended them. Most of them had seen butchery at close quarters

and even those in places of safety who had not been involved had
heard the stories of women mutilated and naked on the ground, of
people hacked to death in their own bungalows then piled on the
wreckage of their furniture and burned. In the prevailing atmosphere of dread, the stories were improved upon without fear of
contradiction and the whole of Northern India was in a state of
terror, with the white men constantly watching their servants or
their soldiers for the slightest move that might suggest treachery,
yet not daring to make a move themselves lest it spark off violence.
It was an atmosphere which could easily lead to too-hasty actions
and was to be the cause of a great deal of tragedy.

The first reinforcements for the beleaguered garrison at Cawnpore had reached Benares on 3 June, before the rising in Cawnpore
had even taken place. They were under the command of Colonel
James George Neill, a harsh capable Scot and a notable leader of
irregular troops who kept himself conscious in the heat on a regimen
of champagne and cold water douches. A man who would not have
been out of place among Cromwell's Puritan soldiers, Neill was a
sincere Christian but was also a man who believed that God helped
those who helped themselves. He was in command of the Madras
Fusiliers, a European regiment of gentlemen rankers, and was on
the point of moving on when reports came in of disturbances at
Azamgarh fifty miles to the north.

Fearing, in the prevailing atmosphere of suspicion, contagion in

Reinforcements crossing
the bridge of boats
at Benares.

75

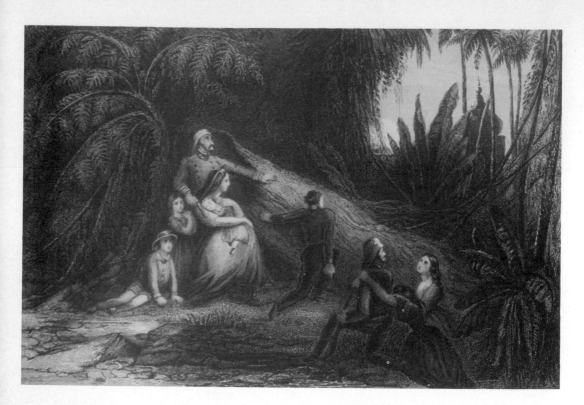

Benares, the most holy city of the Hindu religion, it was decided to
disarm the troops there. By inept handling, however, the disarming
turned into a battle and Neill, who took over from the commanding
officer, to whom the situation and the heat were proving too much,
was not content with suppressing the mutiny but felt that the disaffected people of the district should be shown that British arms
were not as decadent as they thought. Old men, women and
children had their homes burned about their ears and the mutineers
were hunted down 'as though they had been pariah-dogs or jackals'.
Neill was completely absorbed in his task and when an order from
Calcutta reached him ordering him to hurry on to Allahabad, he
telegraphed back, 'Can't move. Wanted here.'

Many were hanged; on one occasion young boys who had done
no more than flaunt rebel colours or beat tom-toms. Volunteer
hanging parties went out into the districts and boasted of the
numbers they had killed, using 'mango trees for gibbets and
elephants for drops.' It was all done in an atmosphere of Christian
self-righteousness. 'God grant,' Neill wrote, 'I may have acted with
justice.'

The justice of his acts was as questionable as the sense, however.
When the news of the trouble in Benares had reached Allahabad,

the civilians had been ordered into the fort for safety, but when nothing happened they had returned to their homes. The officers of the 6th Native Infantry, who comprised part of the garrison, had retained a blind faith in the loyalty of their men, and indeed right up to the last moment their men gave them every reason to expect it, professing indignation at the behaviour of their comrades to the north and even volunteering to march against Delhi. When their offer had been telegraphed to Calcutta, Canning had even begun to believe that the mutiny was confined only to a few stations. Yet a week later, within minutes of a parade at which they had cheered Canning's letter thanking them for their offer, they mutinied and murdered their officers and eight cadets – the youngest only sixteen – who had recently arrived from England.

Their colonel reached the fort by a hair's breadth, his arm shattered and his horse dying. Inside, a company of the same regiment was disarmed through the quick action of Lieutenant Jeremiah Brasyer, a former gardener recently promoted from the ranks for his work in the Sutlej campaigns, who held steady a few doubtful Sikhs and brought up guns with the help of 65 invalids hurried from Chunar by alert civil administrators, and a few hastily armed civilians. Though the fort was secured, however, those Europeans and Eurasians who had left and were caught in the town were slaughtered with as much cruelty and indifference as at Delhi and Meerut, by a mob which included all the sweepings of the gaol; and 1,600 bullocks which had laboriously been collected for the transport of the reinforcements for Cawnpore were lost. The fall of Allahabad virtually sealed Wheeler's fate.

Neill arrived in Allahabad on 11 June, still in plenty of time to relieve Wheeler and soon cleared the city of insurgents. Unfortunately, cholera had struck down many of his men and once again, in the atmosphere of doubt and fear, he considered it his first task to punish the guilty and intimidate the waverers. He fired a portion of the native town and pushed 400 Madras Fusiliers, 300 Sikhs, a detachment of irregular cavalry and two small guns towards Cawnpore, under the command of Major Sydenham Renaud, with instructions to attack and destroy all places occupied by rebels. Renaud interpreted his instructions too literally and burned villages right and left. The need for the co-operation of the local people – without whom the transport required to push on to Cawnpore could not be collected – was forgotten, and the strong measures Neill and Renaud took frightened away the humble peasants and farmers and the labourers who administered to the needs of the army. Neill could still have reached Cawnpore in time

to save Wheeler if he had left Allahabad on the 10th but by the 23rd, two days before the Eurasian woman arrived bringing the Nana Sahib's terms to the entrenchment, he was still not able to march.

The half-caste woman, Mrs Henry Jacobi, who had appeared before Wheeler's entrenchment, carried a message from the Nana Sahib beginning 'To the subjects of Her Most Gracious Majesty Queen Victoria'. It promised a safe passage to Allahabad for all those who had not taken part in the acts of Lord Dalhousie and were prepared to lay down their arms.

It was a hard decision to have to face and, despite his heartbroken condition, Wheeler was at first prepared to hold on until a relief force arrived. There was really no choice, however. The rations were almost exhausted and the women and children were already in a desperate state.

Wheeler left the decision to Captain John Moore and the matter was argued back and forth throughout a sweltering day while Mrs Jacobi was sent back to beg for time. It was finally decided to talk to the rebels and, in the darkness of the evening, Moore left the entrenchment with two other men to conduct the negotiations. It was agreed that, in return for the surrender of their guns and treasure, they should have free exit with their arms and ammunition, and there should be carriages to carry the wounded, women and children to boats which were to be at the riverside ready

provisioned for their journey. The terms were carried to the Nana

Sahib and a messenger brought back his assent, though he insisted that the entrenchment must be evacuated at once. In a fury, Moore said that rather than do so he would fight on and would even blow up his magazine and everybody inside the entrenchment. The Nana Sahib gave way and granted them until dawn. For the first time in weeks they slept in peace, the weary women watching the hungry, exhausted children with thankfulness in their hearts.

Forty large boats were provided at a landing place called the Sati Chowra Ghat, and those which did not have thatched roofs against the sun were hurriedly covered over by coolies. No one was certain how much they could trust the Nana Sahib after his switch of loyalties but three of his aides remained the night in the entrenchment as a symbol of his good faith, while rebel officers who had once admired Wheeler sought him out to express their sorrow at the turn of events. At dawn on 27 June, the survivors, their clothes in rags and stained with dust and blood, gathered their treasures together, digging up boxes of money and silver from the hard earth, while women sewed jewels and spoons into their clothing. Their trunks and boxes long since taken and filled with earth to strengthen the rampart, they had only what they could carry in their hands or on their backs, and they clutched all the tighter to Bibles, locks of hair and other mementoes of relatives who had died. A few of the more cynical like Mowbray Thompson stuffed their pockets and even their hats with cartridges to be on the safe side.

The Nana Sahib appeared to be as good as his word, however, and as the haggard, bandaged defenders and their families waited in a shabby, exhausted group, a procession of sixteen elephants appeared, followed by seventy to eighty palanquins and bullock carts. As the mutineers entered the entrenchment, a few tried to snatch the weapons of the defenders and others attempted to grab jewellery and treasures from the women waiting in the barracks. A sepoy, rebuked by Moore, spat in his face. It was in the minds of several that the whole thing was a trick, especially when the mahouts driving the elephants refused to make the animals kneel to allow their passengers to scramble aboard, but the first groups moved off at 7 am, led by Moore and followed by the line of palanquins carrying the sick and wounded. Bullock carts brought more, while the fit stalked grim-faced alongside, carrying their weapons, their eyes flickering warily over the watching Indians. Although an elephant had been provided for them, Wheeler, his wife and daughters walked.

Where the boats waited, the Ganges ran between high brown banks and it occurred to a few as they arrived that, whether the 79

Nana Sahib honoured his word or not, they could now never get back to the entrenchment. They were in the open, hampered by the sick, women and children, and they no longer had their artillery. There was a cordial exchange of greetings between some of the officers and their old sepoys, however, and enquiries after casualties, while the Indians continued to reassure them they were to leave without harm.

As they moved through a double line of sepoys down to the steps of the ghat and the river, it was seen that nothing had been provided to enable the women and children to get into the boats and there were no means of carrying the sick and wounded aboard, and men and women waded knee-deep in the muddy water while the native boatmen and bearers watched in ominous silence. By 8.30 am the boats were crowded with human beings, panting in the white heat of the morning and taunted constantly from the shore.

They were almost ready to leave when, prompt on nine o'clock, as though at a signal, the boatmen deserted their boats and leapt overboard. Their nerves already on edge and suspecting treachery, the British officers promptly fired on them, and the shots were immediately returned from the trees overhanging the river – so swiftly it seemed the whole thing had been planned. What followed might well have been treachery, because the news of Benares and Allahabad and Neill's terrible reprisals had already been heard by the Indians and there was a feeling of vengeance in the air, yet – though guns had been placed and troops posted – it might still have been pure accident.

'Oh, why are they firing on us?' a terrified child screamed. 'Didn't they promise to leave off?' But the firing increased as the panic-stricken British, caught entirely without shelter, struggled to board the boats. At first the shots had come only from a few mounted troopers of the 2nd Native Cavalry but in no time, as the British replied, a withering fusillade was directed on the boats from the banks and, raked with musketry and cannon, they were set on fire as the sweating, frantic men attempting to push them into midstream were shot down.

Their thatches alight, their occupants jumped into the water, the women screaming and struggling to protect their children from the storm of metal that churned the river to foam. All but three of the boats remained fast, while terrified women and children hid beneath their curved sides among the swirling smoke from the hail of bullets, or waded into deeper water in the hope of escape. As native cavalrymen spurred after them, the wicked sabres, honed to a razor-edge and kept sharp in leather or wooden scabbards, slashed at arms raised to beg for mercy. Wheeler was cut down and fell face-forward in the blood-flecked water, while lighted brands were thrust against the clothing of women, and children were smashed to the ground, their brains dashed out by iron-tipped clubs.

Whether the Nana Sahib was responsible for the massacre or whether it was merely the result of being unable to control his men, at least he now gave orders that it must cease. Wheeler and Moore were already dead, and the men crouching ashore were picking off the pitifully few survivors. As the Nana's message arrived, 60 men and 125 sobbing women and children were dragged ashore, plastered with mud and water and blood, while behind them the bodies floated between the bobbing boats, already hidden beneath the crowding vultures. Only one boat had got away, carrying over 20 people. As it drifted unguided downstream, it ran on to sandbanks and was pushed off again and again by desperate men constantly fired on from the banks by sepoys who kept pace with it. Deciding to die fighting, the few left on board finally struggled ashore, only to be attacked again, and of the seven who managed to plunge into the water to swim for their lives, only four almost naked men reached safety after a three-hour struggle.

Of those left behind at Cawnpore, the men were all killed, while the hysterical women and children were imprisoned in a large house once built by a British officer for his native mistress and known as the Bibigarh, the Lady's House. A few days later they were joined by a few other men and women who had been captured at Fatehgarh. After a gallant defence of the fort in which dummy guns and mines had been constructed, and screws, nuts and bolts had been used as grapeshot, the exhausted garrison there had tried to escape in boats moored under the walls. But they had been seen by sepoys lining the river banks who had shot or cut them down as they ran aground and, shocked, terrified, weeping at the deaths of butchered husbands and children, the survivors were pushed in with the women of Wheeler's garrison.

In two rooms, twenty feet by ten feet, and in conditions which must have been a torment to Victorian modesty, they were fed by sweepers and forced to grind corn for their captors as they tried to make themselves comfortable with only coarse bamboo matting to sleep on and food of unleavened dough and lentil porridge. They had nothing but what they stood up in and fortunately no idea of the horrors that lay ahead.

Chapter 6

The Well
at Cawnpore

While the surviving men at Cawnpore were being butchered and the women were being imprisoned, Havelock's main forces were beginning to reach Allahabad. It was already quite clear that any attempt to relieve Cawnpore and Lucknow would have to be made in strength and Havelock was busy buying spies, gathering thin linen clothing for his British troops, and making sure the defences of Allahabad were safe. Without much help from Neill, who had acquired an inexplicable hatred for the man who had been placed over him, he decided that, though he ought to push on with what he had, he still could not move without transport.

On 3 July, a message was brought in by an exhausted man on a lathered horse that Cawnpore had fallen and that no one was left alive. Two days later a second message arrived to the effect that the Nana Sahib had withdrawn his men and that the Union Jack was now flying over Cawnpore again, and because they wished to believe it, everyone accepted the second message as the genuine one. Havelock, however, had received his news directly from Indian spies sent on by Renaud, and, in no doubt, he passed on to Canning the news that Cawnpore had been lost.

By this time, British rule in the north of India had virtually ceased. Indian soldiers frankly told their officers, 'Sir, we dare not remain loyal', and even maharajahs who had benefited from British friendship found themselves asking their British friends, 'How can your government *ever* survive now?' Even the Punjab was held on faith because every available man had been sent to Delhi. It was the same in Central India, where the Central Indian Agency consisted of six native states, Gwalior, Indore, Dhar and Dewas – ruled by Mahratta princes; and Bhopal and Jawra – Muslim states; with Rajputana, a collection of native states, to the north-west. The only British troops in the area were horse artillery at Mhow, near Indore.

Three hundred miles to the north-east of Mhow was Jhansi, where mutiny had broken out on 5 June, the day when Havelock was telegraphing the news of the fall of Cawnpore. Though the British had taken refuge in the fortress, they had emerged – it was believed on the safe promise of the Rani, that widow of the last ruler who so loathed the British for the annexation of her state – and they had all been murdered. On 8 June, the troops at Nasirabad, in Rajputana, had also mutinied, with the exception of the native cavalry, and had moved off to Delhi. Other mutinies had occurred at Nimach and at Morar in Gwalior, where a contingent of eight

Opposite
The chamber of blood: the scene in the Bibigahr which confronted Havelock's men when they arrived at Cawnpore.

thousand men of the Bengal army had murdered its officers and
their families. At Indore, where the headquarters of the acting
agent, Sir Henry Durand, lay, mutiny had occurred on 1 July and,
though long suspecting trouble, Durand had not been able to
expect help from the British troops at Mhow because they were all
needed to keep that place quiet. He had retired, therefore, to Sihor,
and when the troops at Mhow heard the news from Indore they, too,
had mutinied.

Apart from Simla, Calcutta and a few other places, however, the
crisis had been met with courage and calm if not always with
wisdom. Often, the political agent was distrustful of the sepoys
while the regimental officer was noisily certain he had the confidence of his men. When the civilian had his way, the danger as
often as not passed. When the soldier had his, as often as not the
trouble would begin – probably by his being shot in the back – and
be followed by the inconceivable savagery of indiscriminate
slaughter, with houses on fire, children torn from their mothers'
arms to have their brains dashed out, and women left butchered and
bleeding.

84   The story was the same all over Northern India and there was

hardly one white civilian or soldier whose life was not in peril a dozen times that summer as fleeing people hid in mud huts and drains, even under dunghills, facing months of hunger, humiliation, dirt, hardships, agony, even insanity in the tremendous heat. Such was the emergency, magistrates found themselves riding as cavalry troopers – yet still managing to collect a few taxes or fulfil a few duties when they had time – and one colonel who had sported a handsome black moustache was now seen to have a white one so that it was assumed it had gone white with the horrors he had seen. The explanation was much simpler. He had been in the habit of dyeing it and had not had time in the emergency to make the usual applications.

Many of these men died in battle or, sword in hand, defending their posts, mourned by the simple Indians they had administered. All too often, before they died they were well aware of what their fate was to be and yet they still faced it without flinching, still reading their Bibles, still writing home – 'Unless God in His Mercy interferes, it will be my last' – their letters full of pious demonstrations of their love for their families – 'Kiss my dear Babes for me and tell them how necessary it is for the youngest as well as the oldest to live daily to God.'

There were also incredible cases of Indian devotion – Henry Lawrence's sepoys in the Residency at Lucknow remained true through weeks of appalling dangers and hardship – and strange cases of chivalry. At Shahjahanpur, the British were surprised at their Sunday devotions but, after several had been cut down, other Indian soldiers intervened and the rest were allowed to go – only to be murdered later as they were being sent into Lucknow. All too often they were killed as they took refuge in the only salvation they could think of – prayer.

Some regiments remained faithful due to the isolation of their position or the magnetism of their colonel, but by the end of July almost every unit of the Bengal army that dared do so had mutinied, some to join the Moghul king at Delhi, others to join the sturdier Muslim rising at Lucknow, others still to rally to some minor flag or even simply to behave as bandits, so that the villagers had to arm and organise themselves in self-defence against them and even demand tolls before they would allow them passage through their area. In some cases, the rebels murdered their officers, in others they allowed them to escape. Some units, scrupling to kill them themselves, persuaded others to do it for them. Even among the Indians the Mutiny brought its own kind of horror. Village feuds flared and children were tortured to force them to reveal their

Small bodies of hurriedly raised cavalry learned their duties the hard way in battle.

parents' treasures, and the houses of money-lenders were razed to the ground to destroy all evidence of the debts under which so many Indians lived. Thousands of criminals were released from gutted gaols and the countryside so swarmed with homeless men bent on loot that thousands of Indians fled for protection to whereever the British were still in control.

Even now, there were still such places. Though Robert Tucker, the Commissioner at Fatehpur, died fighting on the roof of his house, his Bible near at hand and within sight of the pillars he had erected bearing the Ten Commandments, in other places where there were good or crafty leaders things held firm. A dozen different methods were used to keep districts loyal. The Commissioner for Jubbulpur printed his own banknotes. Private regiments were raised. One man enlisted criminals and kept them loyal with rebel loot, while another made his regiment into what was in effect a limited company so that his men had the sound reason of profit for remaining loyal. Dozens of minor battles were fought not by regular troops but by groups of unattached men – government officials without districts, officers without regiments, railway workers with-

Lieutenant H. H. Gough
winning the V.C. at
Lucknow.

out jobs, clerks and faithful Indians – armed with weapons which included even hog spears, all of them learning their duties quickly by the hardest of ways. In Benares, Robert Tucker's brother, Henry, the Commissioner, with his judge and his magistrate, had faced the danger 'without moving a muscle', even riding unarmed with his daughter in the most exposed places, confident in his Bible and the thought that 'The Lord is my rock, my fortress and my deliverer.' There had been no scenes of horror in Benares beyond what Neill had wrought. At Arrah, the problems were different and 66 men, because they behaved with foresight and energy, were to hold out for eight days against thousands until they were relieved.

The first moves to bring rescue and retribution were being made, however. Troops had already arrived at Delhi and Havelock was at last moving out of Allahabad, setting off for the north only four days after hearing of Wheeler's death. Small, prim, dressed in a plain blue frock coat, he announced to his men that they were setting out to 'avenge the fate of British men and women'. Led by five pipers of the 78th Highlanders and the band of the Madras Fusiliers and threatened with the onset of the monsoons, his force consisted of only 1,200 men, many of them only nervous teenagers with no experience of war. The Sikhs were led by Brasyer, the ex-gardener who had held them steady at Allahabad, and the cavalry consisted of only twenty civilians and unattached officers under Captain Lousada Barrow, but Havelock ruled them with the iron rod of an Old Testament general, arresting officers who did not

At Arrah 66 men held out for eight days against thousands of mutineers.

Opposite
The Mutiny as seen by an unknown Indian artist.

89

Havelock's attack on
the Nana Sahib
at Fatehpur.

implicitly obey the strict orders he had imposed to avoid straggling
or the giving away of his position, and not allowing for one moment
any of the old casual habits of march to hinder him in getting his
small column in motion.

As they left, the rains broke and the road became a quagmire of
knee-deep, steaming slush. In front and on either side in the hot
Indian sun, they saw a vast and dreary wasteland loud with the
noise of frogs and crickets and dotted with the ruins of forsaken
villages and gutted rest-houses, with here and there a dead body
that had been gnawed by wild pigs. Renaud had put to death every
man he might possibly suspect and Havelock's soldiers marched
between lines of corpses hanging from the trees.

Five days later, trudging along the line of the Grand Trunk
Road, they caught up with Renaud then, at Batinda, near Fatehpur, they had their first brush with the enemy. As they prepared
breakfast, they were fired on by rebels who, not realising that
Renaud's small force had been supplemented by Havelock's
column, were deploying for the attack. Delaying as much as possible
to give his weary men as much rest as he could, Havelock merely
posted one hundred riflemen and eight guns under Captain Maude
in a copse ahead of his position and, disposing his infantry in line of
column just behind, with Irregulars on the left and Volunteer
Cavalry on the right, he awaited the attack of men driven to a
frenzy of enthusiasm by Wheeler's defeat.

As they approached, Maude's guns opened fire and when Tantia Topi, the Nana Sahib's military adviser and commander of his bodyguard, had the elephant on which he was riding brought down by a round shot, the rebels fled, leaving behind all their baggage, twelve guns and ammunition and a great deal of treasure. It had been a victory for the Enfield rifle. Its fire, reaching out to the rebels at an unexpected distance, according to Havelock 'filled them with dismay'. Though Renaud's Irregulars had proved unreliable and were disbanded, there had been few British casualties, and most of them were from sunstroke. 'Thanks to Almighty God, who gave me victory,' Havelock wrote '. . . I now march to retake Cawnpore.'

The first stroke of vengeance had been successful.

Granting his men a day's rest, Havelock pushed on again, and by 15 July he was only 33 miles from Cawnpore. On this day he fought two more battles. He captured a rebel-held village at Aong and, pressing on to the Panda Nudi River in an attempt to capture a stone bridge before it was blown up to prevent his crossing, he drove his force on while the bearers were still collecting up the wounded at Aong. After an artillery duel, the troops swarmed forward to the bridge just as a charge laid by the rebels went up with a roar. Though the parapet broke, the bridge held and the rebels fled.

Though he did not know it then, Havelock's victories had sealed the fate of the five men and 206 women and children held prisoner in the Bibigarh. Exulting in the defeat of Wheeler, the Nana Sahib had had himself proclaimed Peshwa, or ruler of the Mahrattas. He was not having an easy time, however. The tradesmen of the city, groaning under the depredations of the mutineers, execrated him as the author of their sufferings while the sepoys complained of his niggardliness in rewarding them for their services and threatened that if he did not appear among them they would fetch him. On 5 July they put their threat into execution and he moved his headquarters from a tent to the Old Cawnpore Hotel, only thirty yards from where the women were imprisoned.

When on 15 July, the news came in that the Nana Sahib's force had been twice defeated and that Havelock, with the terrible Neill not far behind, was within a day's march of the city, the Nana Sahib began to realise that if he were defeated again, the captives in the Bibigarh could furnish the British with damning evidence

against him. If they were put out of the way, however, Havelock might consider there was nothing to be gained by advancing against the city. A group of sepoys from the 6th Native Infantry, the regiment which had murdered the cadets at Allahabad, were sent to do the job. They were not prepared to murder women and children, though, and fired their weapons into the ceiling. According to Corporal William Forbes-Mitchell, of the 93rd Highlanders, who heard the story later from Tantia Topi, the Nana Sahib's lieutenant, it was one of the Nana Sahib's enemies, a girl from his zenana who wished to see him irretrievably implicated, who procured five men willing to do what the rebellious sepoys had refused to do. They arrived outside the Bibigarh that evening, all carrying tulwars.

It had long since been noted by British cavalry officers that these Indian swords were often old British sabres honed to razor sharpness, and cavalry experts had noticed that in battle a backward swing with one of them was enough to cut a man in half, even through his pouch and ammunition, and that, dropped across a man's hands as they lay on the reins, they were capable of lopping them clean off. Of the five men, two were Muslims and butchers by trade, two were Hindu peasants and the last was one of the Nana's bodyguard. Between them they murdered every man, woman and child in the Bibigarh. There was one solitary survivor, a man called Shepherd, who had left the lines to try to get help disguised as an Indian cook and had been captured. Overlooked in the confusion, he was found later in a dungeon in the city, fettered, filthy and half-starved.

Hearing there were British women and children still alive in Cawnpore, Havelock roused his men on the 16th and, as they assembled in the dark, he addressed them with the usual call to the Almighty. 'By God's help,' he said, 'we will save them, or every man will die in the attempt,' and, cheering, they set off. Not 25 miles away in Cawnpore were almost 10,000 of the Nana Sahib's troops.

Unable to proceed faster than the slow-trudging bullocks pulling their waggons and guns, they halted on the 16th at a village called Maharajpur, just outside Cawnpore, where the men breakfasted on dry biscuits and porter. A spy had arrived with an outline of the Nana Sahib's positions which lay three miles ahead in a wide curve screened by mango groves and mud-walled villages. The force moved off again in the early afternoon, without baggage, sick or wounded. The sun was scorchingly hot and the metal of their weapons burned their fingers. In their thick clothing, the heat played havoc with the Highlanders and one man after another reeled from the ranks. The country was an area of rice fields, flat and featureless except for clumps of palms, and just beyond a forked road they saw the enemy, their bands playing English tunes, waiting for them with seven guns and strongpoints among the native villages.

While Barrow's tiny force of cavalry trotted forward to occupy their attention, the Madras Fusiliers moved through groves of mangoes to right and left. As the rebel fire smashed through the trees to bring down a shower of branches and leaves and force the infantry to lie down, Maude's guns raked the enemy battery. The mutineers' guns were far too big for the British weapons, however, and Havelock had no option but to send his men forward in a wall of flesh and blood. As the orders rang out, the line of Highlanders rose to their feet. They had already marched twenty miles that day and they now drove across the open ground into the teeth of the guns, while the grape and case shot lashed the water of the paddy-fields to foam and tore great holes in their ranks. When they failed to halt them, the enemy gunners began to lose their nerve and, trying to fire too fast, fired too high and, to the music of the pipes, the men leapt forward.

Skewering the gunners, bending their bayonets in their fury and hammering down all resistance with the butts of their weapons, they rolled up the rebel flank, and as they halted, panting, the battery silenced, to reform by a small bridge, another storm of fire came on them from the centre of the Indian position. Havelock spurred his horse forward and the charge carried the Highlanders through the guns and the scattered white-clad bodies and out on to the Grand Trunk Road where the twenty volunteer horsemen did the rest.

The battle appeared to be over, but suddenly the retreating rebels faced about and their bands struck up a defiant tune. The Nana Sahib was seen riding from point to point, and another great gun, surrounded by a force of rebels now reinforced to ten thousand, fired on the British. Maude was unable to make his exhausted bullocks drag his artillery forward again, and Havelock, seeing the crisis of the battle had arrived, gave the order for the final charge. 'Another charge . . . wins the day,' he said. The Highlanders went forward once more, while the 84th and the 64th advanced on the vast gun. Young Harry Havelock, the general's son, in the lead, drove his horse deliberately for the muzzle and, despite the astonishing precision of the rebels' fire, the British pressed grimly towards the Nana's position.

Opposite
A shamshir belonging to the son of the King of Delhi.

93

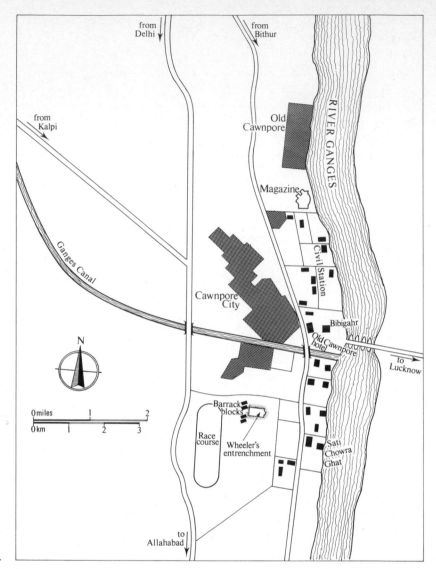

Cawnpore.

The ground in their rear was strewn with dead and dying men but their steady advance finally unnerved the rebels and, as they cheered and made their final dash for the gun, the enemy began to break. The Nana Sahib was among the first away, spurring towards Bithur, carrying with him thousands of its inhabitants, terrified by the news that the infuriated British were just behind. There were still a few gunners by the great weapon but the British were now close on them, purple in the face with the heat and the effort of running fully loaded. The last round screamed over them as they reached within a hundred yards then they rose and poured

94

in a shattering volley, and swept forward into the enemy positions.

As Maude's guns came up at last, the rebels fled and the men stood around Havelock cheering in a spasm of hysterical excitement, relief and thankfulness. They were still two miles from Cawnpore but with darkness coming on they could only lie down, with little to eat and – with their baggage five miles to the rear – nothing to cover them. On the following morning, the 17th, they marched into Cawnpore as the Nana's troops streamed out at the other side.

The advanced guard of one hundred dusty men of the 84th Foot under Captain Henry Ayton, filthy with sweat and the grime of battle, were first into the city. When they reached the Bibigarh and saw the horror inside, they could not speak. It looked as though cattle had been slaughtered in there. The walls were covered with bloody hand-prints and the floor with fragments of human limbs, clothing, Bibles, shoes, trinkets and lockets containing hair. A brief diary written on a piece of notepaper in a woman's hand was also found. It ran: 21 May, Went into the barrack; 5 June, Cavalry mutinied; 6 June, First shot fired; 17 June, Aunt Lily died (Mrs W. Lindsay); 18 June, Uncle Willie died (Major W. Lindsay); 27 June, George died (Ensign G. Lindsay); 27 June, Left the barrack; 29 June [sic], Taken out of the boats; . . . 9 July, Alice died; 12 July, Mama died (Mrs G. Lindsay). The daughter herself had died with the rest on 15 July. The severed heads and limbs and mutilated bodies had been thrown into a well close by, which was filled to within six feet of the top. 'I have faced death in every form,' one man wrote, 'but I could not look down that well again.'

Colonel John Alexander Ewart, with the 78th Highlanders, searching for his cousin and namesake and his family, found himself by Wheeler's entrenchment. The rooms of the barracks were full of books but contained no clue to the fate of the defenders except a message scrawled on a wall to the effect that Captain Halliday, of the 56th Native Infantry, had been killed by a round shot. Moving towards the Bibigarh, he found the trees about it covered with sabre cuts, as though the victims had tried to hide behind them, and under a bush he found the head of a pretty girl of eighteen. He was swept up in a feeling of utter rage. The blood still caked the floor and several of the prisoners after being murdered had been hung on a gibbet close by. His cousin, who had been badly wounded in the entrenchment, had been killed by men of his own regiment as he was carried to the river. His wife had been murdered and of their small daughter there was no news whatsoever.

Chapter 7

England Expects

With the well at Cawnpore, the British flung aside any restraint they had shown up to that point. Ewart's reaction was typical. A veteran of the Crimea where he had been among the first to try to save the wounded after the charge of the Light Brigade, he said he felt 'all feeling of mercy or consideration for the mutineers' leaving him. He felt he was 'no longer a Christian' and all he wanted was revenge, and he admitted that, while in the Crimea he had never wished to kill a Russian, now his one idea was to kill every rebel he came across.

'I can never spare a sepoy again,' said Neill. 'All that fall into my hands will be dead men.' Captured mutineers were forced to wipe up the bloodstains in the Bibigarh, and the task, Neill ordered, was to be made as revolting to the feelings of the captives as possible. High-caste Brahmins were even made to lick up the blood, then, before they could indulge in any ceremony of purification after this defilement of caste, he shot or hanged them, while Muslims were sewn up in pigskins and smeared with hog fat before being killed.

Neill assumed that all mutineers were guilty of the massacre of the women. As far as the massacre at the boats was concerned, this rough judgement was fair enough, but the only mutineers concerned with the women in the Bibigarh had actually refused to indulge in murder. But this was not known at the time and Neill was sure of the guidance of God. 'I cannot help seeing His finger in all this,' he wrote. He was kept under control while Havelock was in Cawnpore but when Havelock left, he tortured and killed his captives without even bothering to make sure they were guilty.

When the news of Meerut and Delhi reached England the first reactions were sheer disbelief. India was 'the brightest gem in the British crown' and no one believed that the British troops there were not equal to the emergency. It was accepted, of course, that there had been casualties, but as they began to learn of whole families being wiped out – one man alone was reported to have lost 32 relatives – they realised this was more than a mere minor uprising of natives, and the mood changed. And when the detailed reports of Cawnpore came in and those stories which had not been believed originally began to be accepted, there was a shrill call for vengeance, immediate and blood-red. The attitude startled the more moderate. 'Not one man in ten seems to think that the hanging and shooting of 40,000 or 50,000 men could be otherwise than practicable and right,' Canning reported to the Queen. Victoria, who had always disliked the arrogant term 'nigger' for her subjects in India, could only feel sorrow and indignation at the un-Christian

Opposite
Brigadier-General James George Neill.

97

spirit that was being shown under the cloak of Christianity and religion.

Since the Victorians shrank from all coarse physical facts, newspapers only hinted at the atrocities, saying they were 'too horrible to mention'. So wild and quite untrue stories of rape spread, despite the fact that contact with a white Christian would have been considered defilement to a Hindu.

In the growing atmosphere of hatred and revenge no one seemed to remember that the massacres had been roundly condemned by many Indians of all classes. They had accepted the Englishman's salt, these Indians felt, as a token of friendship, and they considered it shocking to be faithless to one's salt; it was this, in fact, as much as anything else, which ensured that the rebellion did not develop into a national uprising. But only a few British were in a position – or, for that matter, in a frame of mind – to find out what the Indians felt, and their cries of outrage only served as a spur to men who thought like Neill. Today there is a tendency to regard the British reprisals as a matter for shame, but history must be judged by the standards of its own period and, seen through the eyes of the Victorians, they assume a different aspect. Campaigns have an emotion and an atmosphere of their own, and the Indian Mutiny, because of the women and children involved, had a special sense of horror and dread. To be taken prisoner by either side invariably meant death, and 'Vengeance' became the *cri de coeur*.

With the stock market shaking and world opinion solidly against the rebels, the British reached for God as justification for every battle and every slaughter that was perpetrated.

To the uneducated private soldiers who were in the forefront of danger there was never any question of what the whole thing was about. Though in their ranks there were the sons of impoverished officers trying to win their commissions the hard way and intelligent, well-read men well able to set down their thoughts with clarity and conciseness, for the most part the soldiers' actions were dictated by the unthinking dogmas of the slums. On the whole they had been recruited in the narrow streets and round the inns and brothels of London, Manchester and other great cities. They had joined the army because they were hungry and a regiment provided security and a roof over their heads; a large number of them were illiterate Irish peasants driven from home by the famines of the late 'Forties. There was a remarkable regard for their officers, but little was ever done by the authorities for their comfort and they looked on war as a means of enriching themselves with loot and as a change from the boring squalor of their lives. A victory as often as not meant liquor and, while they were still capable of a rough and ready honour and a remarkable gentleness at times to women or a wounded friend, they were never likely to question the whys and wherefores of the struggle in India. To the ordinary soldier, with the example of his elders and betters before him, the Mutiny was a simple conflict between God and the Forces of Darkness, between Christ and the evils of Hinduism and Muslimism. The Mutiny, in effect, had very quickly become a religious war with all the fanaticism attendant on such wars.

Nevertheless, the mutineers *were* all along guilty of an offence which was already legally punishable by death, and there was no legality about the slaughter of the civilian populations at Allahabad, Cawnpore, Delhi and other places. There is also plenty of evidence that the bazaars had soon had enough of the mutineers and the arrogance and cruelty they showed even to their own kind, and it was not long before the Indians in these cities were longing for the rule of law again.

Unfortunately, this attitude did not last long. Neither the British nor the Punjabis hurrying to Delhi made much distinction between one Indian and another. They were all traitors – even feeble old women, who, as one soldier said, were 'the beggars as breeds 'em' – and those who were totally innocent of atrocities, whether they sympathised with or feared the mutineers, when they were swept up in the net of reprisal, ended up bewildered, terrified and bitter, imprisoned without trial, occasionally as at Ajnala near Amritsar, dying in overcrowded cells as bad as the Black Hole of Calcutta. There were no recriminations. 'England,' it was said, 'expected every man to do his duty.'

The British attitude was common almost everywhere. John Nicholson, Deputy Commissioner of the Peshawar Division and a good churchman who after the battle of Gujerat had allowed his prisoners to go home quietly, wrote 'I would inflict the most excruciating tortures on them with a perfectly easy conscience.' Even wholesale castration was talked of and a young man at the Cambridge Union was applauded when he said, 'When every bayonet is red with blood, when every gibbet creaks beneath its ghastly burden; when the ground in front of every cannon is strewn with rags and flesh and shattered bone – then talk of mercy.'

One of the causes for the fury was the sense of betrayal. To the officers of the Bengal army, the mutiny was a psychological horror as they saw the men they loved turn on them. They had regarded 99 their Indian soldiers as friends and women had felt it safe to travel long distances alone with them, or to allow their children to play with their sepoy guards. But now suddenly these friends had become murderous unreasoning enemies and the British also abandoned themselves to unreason. The suddenness of the treachery only served to make it worse, together with the fact that for the first time in generations Englishwomen and children had been exposed to the attack of foreigners in war. The Victorian Englishman had raised his womenfolk to a pedestal and, their danger struck to the heart of the English soldier's emotions. When a child was born in a wagon in the camp at Delhi, a soldier remarked that they had received their first reinforcement to a force that was formed 'to avenge the blood of innocents'.

The same cries for vengeance that Havelock's men uttered at Cawnpore were being repeated at Delhi as the British had begun to return. As they set up their tents they could see the dark, stripped bodies of the mutineers shining with sweat as they worked over their guns, and the first thing they found was a cart containing the putrefying bodies of Colonel Ripley's officers of the 54th, which had been covered for lack of anything else with women's dresses taken from a looted house. It had been abandoned near the Flagstaff Tower and forgotten in the hurried flight a month before.

Confidence was beginning to return a little by this time, however, and men on leave in the hills began to hurry back to their units to be in the forefront of any attack. They were moved by the desire for revenge and the knowledge that promotion always came more quickly in wartime. They had taken tearful leave of wives and there had been tender partings from sweethearts, taken as custom demanded on one knee while they exchanged sentimental keepsakes and photographs that had been prayed over long and earnestly. Others, more concerned with vengeance, looked sternly on the likenesses of murdered relatives and solemn oaths were sworn across the blades of swords. They were all certain that, once the British were back at Delhi, the mutineers would throw in their hand and the place would fall quickly. But as they gathered together, a far more deadly enemy than the mutineers began to strike at them. While they did not lack food or even comforts such as beer or wine, in the tremendous heat many of them were wide-open to sunstroke and heatstroke because they were often still wearing high-collared scarlet jackets and even brass helmets which

Men on leave in the
hills hurried to
join their units.

became so hot their wearers died of apoplexy. And now cholera,
that scourge which had struck down the Commander-in-Chief, also
began to take its toll.

Despite their concern with morals and piety, the Victorians
never paid much attention to hygiene. The disease that had already
claimed Anson sprang from bad sanitation and was airborne or
waterborne and manifested itself first in the form of diarrhoea and
vomiting and then in muscle-cramps and finally asphyxia. There
had been an epidemic in Europe lasting from 1847 to 1855 which
had decimated the armies in the Crimea, and asiatic cholera had
its home in India, particularly in the lowlands of Bengal where the
Mutiny had broken out.

The ground was so hard, however, it was difficult to dig graves
and the animals which had been killed also presented a special
problem. As often as not they were left in the sun until they swelled
and burst, and finally dissolved in a mass of indescribable putrefaction which bred flies and filled the air with their terrible smell.

By this time, a vast area of tents had begun to spring up behind
the arid, soil-less, dusty Ridge, and, despite the difficulties, the
British were beginning to look forward to finishing the job. They
had taken on a tremendous task, however. There were seven miles
of wall round the city, 24-foot-high and with a vast ditch 25-foot
wide in front. The gates were protected by 40 guns and strongpoints, to say nothing of 114 guns, many of them vast 24-pounders,

mounted on the walls. Against them the British could muster only 2,900 troops and 22 light field guns. And while the British held the 60-foot-high Ridge commanding the northern side of the city, the other side, against the river, was not even properly invested so that the mutineers could constantly be reinforced. They were heard again and again arriving by the bridge of boats, their bands playing British tunes they had learned like 'Cheer, Boys, Cheer', 'The Girl I Left Behind Me', and 'Auld Lang Syne', even, on occasions 'God Save The Queen'. What it amounted to really was that it was the besiegers who were besieged.

Nevertheless, outposts were built at the Flagstaff Tower and other points, while the main body remained behind the Ridge; and from in front of the gutted cantonments overlooking the baked brown earth of the area towards the city, cracked by ravines and dry stream beds and choked with brushwood, the British guns and mortars began one after another to hammer at the city walls, sometimes from a distance of only one thousand yards. Between them lay the buildings, gardens, mosques, tombs and huts among the thick trees and mangoes, where not long before British families had hidden in terror on the day of the outbreak. The ruins were surrounded by orange, lime and rose trees which threw a blaze of colour across the tawny earth, and the charred British bungalows were already overgrown with creeper. However, there was a canal handy, containing drinkable water, which was fortunate because the River Jumna, a confusion of channels, sandbanks and lagoons here and there bordered by mangroves and malarial swamps, was too foul and the wells were all stuffed with corpses.

There were constant alarms in the darkness and in the confused area of broken ground, as the rebels tried to take advantage of the British weakness. But the attacks were all thrown back, and among those who emerged as natural leaders were Hodson and Colonel James Hope Grant, a lanky Scot in command of the 9th Lancers and the Guides, a man who was always energetic and 'never better than when he has lots to do'. The temperature in the tents sometimes reached 110 degrees Fahrenheit, however, and before long it was only the thought of the approaching rains that made life bearable as they panted inside them – under their beds at times for extra protection from the sun. Prostrated by the heat, as Europeans they had never hitherto had to endure much of it.

Sunday was not missed, however, and services and prayer meetings were held without fail, and pious and compassionate officers scourged themselves as they struggled to apportion blame for the
mutinies. 'Our great sin has been in paying too much attention to

General Sir James
Hope Grant

their religion and too little to our own . . .' one of them wrote. 'I look upon this business in the light of a heavy punishment for the ungodly . . . lives the greater part of us have lived in India.' Nevertheless, some of the more sprightly youngsters, indifferent to who was to blame and concerned only with staying alive and cheerful, contrived to get some fun, fishing in the canal when they could with a bottle of beer for a prize, or playing tennis in the garden of some abandoned house, attended all the time by their Indian servants, who carried meals to them when they were on duty – even through shell fire and often arriving with the crockery chipped by splinters.

Fresh troops sent by John Lawrence from the Punjab continued to arrive, some of them wild and newly-loyal Afghans from the northern frontier, some of them mercenary Gurkhas from Nepal, many of them having marched hundreds of miles. But speed was important and so were men, and it was necessary to raise still more troops. Among those asked to help was Hodson who raised a force of irregular horse from hard-riding Sikhs. Because of their scarlet turbans, they became known as the Flamingoes, but as Hodson's Horse they were to become one of the most famous regiments in the Indian Army. Then his old regiment, the Guides, arrived. They had marched six hundred miles from the Punjab to Delhi in three 103

weeks and, to the amazement of the onlookers, they proceeded to mob him in their delight at seeing him again. More men were daily expected from Cawnpore where Wheeler's fate was still unknown and, unaware of what had happened, the besiegers waited – and waited – growing more weary each day of the discomfort of the camp on the rocky Ridge and of watching their friends die.

There was little organisation and they were plagued as much by their commanders as by the enemy. Major-General Reed arrived to take over the command of the force on 10 June but he was senile and enfeebled – 'a poor infirm old man', one officer described him '. . . a puff of wind would carry him away' – and he was so knocked up by the heat on arrival he had to take to his bed immediately and was unable to assume executive command which remained where it was. Reed's illness however seemed to affect Barnard. New to the country and overcome by his responsibility, he was brave enough but like so many more he was also too old, and was considered by Reed's critic to be 'as fit to command as the Pope of Rome'. Major Laughton, his senior engineer, was occupied with a beautiful young Persian wife and couldn't have cared less about Delhi, while Archdale Wilson, his chief of artillery, was always against any undertaking for which he might be held responsible if it went wrong.

Morale sagged and men became indifferent about their appearance, one unit being known as 'The Dirty Shirts'. In the main, the British now wore clothing dyed khaki with curry powder or mud,

but the rebels, having abandoned their British uniforms, usually wore white, and 'it was a pretty sight to see them . . .' one officer noted enviously on the occasion of a sortie, 'their arms glittering, pennons flying, and their whole appearance . . . a garish contrast to the . . . dingy dress of their foes.'

Because of the vacillation of the senior officers, the course of events was determined, as one staff officer wrote, by the conduct of the besieged rather than by the councils of the besiegers, and some of the younger men began to consider that it was up to them to nudge their superiors into action. The Kabul and Lahore gates of the city were not yet bricked up and the bridges over the ditch had not yet been cut down, and eager and enthusiastic young sappers began to advocate a dawn attack on them. Such an attack could well end in disaster, however. There were 150,000 people in the city and, as Barnard gloomily warned Lord Canning on 13 June, if he suffered a reverse it could be fatal because he had no reserves. Hodson was as good at organising intelligence as he was at carrying it, though, and the information his spies brought indicated that the enemy's real strength lay between 40,000 and 60,000, only a proportion of them trained soldiers, and that their leaders were completely at loggerheads. Despite the odds, indecision by the British could only make the situation worse.

Certainly the mutineers were running riot in the city, half-drunk, looting, lighting fires in the streets, even bursting into the palace to

Hodson's Horse in action.

105

insult the king, whom they suspected, with good reason, of trying to come to terms with the British. Nevertheless, with every day the British delayed, they grew more powerful and more confident. They had fully expected to be punished for Meerut and Delhi and with every hour that went by they began to feel they never would be. And as they grew more bold and more excited and the city merchants began to bury their treasures and lock their doors, Hodson and a few others grew vociferous for attack. In sheer desperation Barnard told them to make a plan. 'Times must be changed,' Hodson thought dryly, 'when four subalterns are called upon to suggest a means of carrying out so vital an enterprise as this!'

The plan was a bold one – a young man's plan – and left the Ridge virtually unguarded, and it might just have succeeded because the rebels were completely unaware of what was afoot. But, through lack of staff know-how among the planners it ended in a fiasco. It was ordered for dawn on 13 June, but no one remembered to explain what was happening to the senior officers, and when an excited subaltern raced up at the last minute to Brigadier Graves, the man on whom the first responsibility for Delhi had fallen on the day of the outbreak, and asked him to withdraw the hundreds of soldiers on picket duty along the Ridge, he thought the man had gone mad. By the time the matter was explained, it was too late. To the fury of the planners there was no alternative but to call the attack off, and the senior officers settled down once more to wait for reinforcements.

The fighting continued in the brassy heat haze, still dictated by the rebels who attempted to attack the British camp, and there were bloody scuffles in the dark as rebel cavalry swept down roads left unguarded because of the shortage of men. The rains still held off and they were sickened by the smell of the vast carcasses of dead elephants and camels which no one had yet thought to move, and by the stench of human bodies in their shallow graves. News came in of disasters in other parts of the country – Bareilly, Gwalior and Jhansi – and on the anniversary of the Battle of Plassey, twenty thousand rebels, harangued by their leaders, streamed out of the city, once more wearing their red coats and their British medals, and the fight went on until evening in the scorching heat. The rebel gunners had been well trained and, with the British guns smaller and their gunners slower, did a great deal of damage. So low was the morale of the British troops by now that they refused to leave shelter and it was the officers who loaded and fired the guns to drive the rebels back.

It seemed as though the siege was never-ending and the condition

of the British appeared to be growing worse. Their camp had become a permanent city of canvas, with bazaars, thatched huts and
thousands of bullocks, camels and horses, in an area swept bare for
forage so that nothing but stunted trees remained among the rocky
hollows. They were still worried about their supply lines and were
short of ammunition for their 24-pounders. Having to fire back the
shot that came from the mutineers' guns, they offered a reward of
half a rupee to the camp followers who brought them in. Sometimes
the native servants were too quick, though, and forgot that the
shots were hot and, as they ran to pick them up, they had to drop
them again and dance about, blowing on their fingers.

The British did not even entirely trust the Punjabis and the
Sikhs who had arrived among them, and lives continued to be lost
through disease and thrown away because of inadequate defences
and lack of organisation. On duty sometimes for three days at a
stretch, they were plagued by fever and prickly heat and by flies
which 'literally darkened the air, descending in myriads and covering everything . . . Foul and loathsome they were.' As they settled
on eyes, lips and food, everyone knew that they had fattened on the
putrid corpses of men and animals which lay unburied in all directions. With little known about hygiene, kitchens and even water

The mutineers in Delhi
ran riot, looting and
even bursting into the
King's Palace.

107

tanks were placed near cess pits and the diseases spread. The air was tainted with corruption and the heat intense, and a bottle of ale became the sweetest draught a man could think of. The fighting continued, minor engagements for the most part, but men still collapsed in them of apoplexy and heatstroke, yet, because the Commissariat refused to pay dhooly bearers, all too often they were left in the sun to die, 'their faces turning quite black in a few minutes'.

On 24 June, however, new heart was put into the little force by the arrival of Brigadier Neville Chamberlain, who was considered to be an intelligent, resolute man, and then as Colonel Richard Baird Smith, an energetic imaginative engineer, replaced the apathetic Laughton, spirits began to rise. The long expected rains came at last but, as the camp became a quagmire, they were found to be probably worse than the heat. Corpses were washed out of the earth and the air became oppressive and it was no longer possible to sleep outside. On 5 July, the cholera struck down Barnard and, with his successor, Reed, still an invalid, Chamberlain became virtually in command. But he was badly wounded during a rebel attack on 14 July, and, when Reed decided, after a mere twelve days in control, to return to the hills for his health, the command devolved on Archdale Wilson. Like all the rest he unhesitatingly put his trust in God. 'This is a fearful responsibility,' he wrote to his wife ' . . . but the Lord God in whom I put my trust will surely give me strength and support.'

Wilson was never an impressive figure as a commander but, despite his vacillation, he was not too old to have lost his bodily activity and he did have considerable ability as an organiser. Though he remained unpopular and distrusted, conditions began to improve at once and morale rose further as he brought order into dress and a little pride into units. By 29 July, the besiegers were beginning to feel that the tide was turning and, with reports of the bankers and citizens of Delhi praying for the return of the British, the younger officers once more decided that the time had come to make an assault.

There was no such feeling of optimism at Lucknow.

It was a difficult city in which to prepare a defence and William Howard Russell, the correspondent of *The Times*, who had made his name in the Crimea and was in India to inform the British people of what was happening there, wrote of it later that it was

'a vision of palaces'. Azure and golden domes, he said, cupolas, colonnades, façades of pillars and columns, terraced roofs – all rose above the bright green of the verdure. For miles it seemed to spread, from the centre to the outlying palaces and summer houses, golden spires glittering in the sun with turrets and golden domes. To Russell it seemed a city 'more vast than Paris . . . and more brilliant'. The Residency area, which included offices as well as the homes of officials, stood to the north of the city on its raised plateau, backing on to the river Gumti. Further upriver was the old fort, the Machchi Bewan, in which there was still a garrison and an arsenal.

Lucknow . . . 'a vision of palaces'.

Although by resolute leadership and commonsense, Lawrence had avoided the butchery of Meerut and Delhi, there had been little time for preparations and not as much had been done as might have been. There were still houses overlooking the defensive area which had not been demolished, and buildings within 25 yards of the perimeter which rebels could fortify and loophole or use as bases from which mines might be driven under the defences. So far, however, despite isolated incidents and local risings and the murder of a few officers, no attempt had been made against the Europeans in Lucknow itself.

Lawrence was by no means deluded that he was safe, though: he was well aware that British rule in Oudh had virtually ceased to exist. The families from the outposts had arrived in the city now. They had slept in their stations with loaded pistols and swords under their pillows in an atmosphere of knife-edged suspense. Fearing all the way that the sepoys who escorted them would murder them, the women had arrived in palanquins and carts and on the backs of elephants, exhausted, dusty, parched and terrified. The

109

quarters they had been given in the Residency had shocked them because they seemed neither wholesome nor safe and contained not a scrap of furniture and, with the hottest period of the year upon them, they were already having to endure swarms of flies and mosquitoes.

The loyal remnants of those native regiments which had mutinied had been incorporated into the garrison, together with a few elderly pensioners but, while he was ready for whatever might come, on 12 June, Lawrence had written, 'Every outpost, I fear, has fallen, and we daily expect to be besieged by the confederated mutineers and their allies.'

The fortification of the Residency area had continued without halt but Lawrence by now had begun to believe that if only Delhi could be taken and Cawnpore could hold out they would be spared the horrors of a siege. Towards the end of June, however, on the day that the news of the Cawnpore massacre arrived, the information came in that the mutineers were concentrating at Nawabganj, 25 miles to the north-east. Lawrence had only 927 British officers and men and 700 loyal sepoys to guard the Residency with its 700 non-combatant coolies and 600 women and children, but Martin Gubbins, the Financial Commissioner – a man with a vehement force of will and an immense courage which occasionally degenerated into rashness and insubordination – demanded a decisive blow against the mutineers, whom he claimed consisted of only 500 foot, 500 horse and one gun. Not entirely convinced of the rebels' small numbers, ill with overwork and with little military experience, nevertheless Lawrence decided to lead against them a force of 300 of the 32nd Foot, 170 Native Infantry, 36 Volunteer Horse, the 84th Oudh Irregular Cavalry with 10 guns and a howitzer drawn by an elephant, and meet them at Chinhut, 10 miles from Lucknow.

The force moved off at dawn on 30 June but, due to the bad staff work that plagued all Victorian armies, most of them had had nothing to eat. After a march in the scorching heat, a halt was called for breakfast at the Kokrail where there was a bridge over the river, but unfortunately, the rations had been forgotten and the men were already exhausted and desperately hungry. Riding forward, Lawrence examined the country ahead with a telescope but could see nothing and had just sent back a message ordering a withdrawal to Lucknow when he suddenly saw a large body of men moving forward in front of him. Countermanding his order at once, he instructed his troops to advance and, after another mile and a half, they came unexpectedly on the enemy 1,200 yards away, their wings covered by villages, their centre astride the road. As the

Sir John Lawrence.

English appeared the rebel artillery opened fire at once.

Against the small British force there were 5,500 infantry, 800 horse and over a dozen heavy guns, and their leader, Barhat Ahmed, was a far better soldier than Lawrence. After a cannonade of an hour, the rebels began to advance and pour into the village of Ismailganj, which enabled them to direct their fire against the British flank. The other wing was also being threatened now and at this moment the dubious native cavalry with Lawrence and the native gunners manning six of his guns chose to desert. An attempt to retake Ismailganj failed and the enemy cavalry began to encircle the forces still remaining to him. A retreat was ordered over the river while Lawrence's Volunteer Horse drove at the enemy cavalry. With his ammunition exhausted, Lawrence could only resort to bluff and he placed guns on the bridge and posted the gunners over them with their port-fires lighted. The danger of attacking a battery, apparently fully loaded, over a narrow bridge, was just too much for the mutineers and their hesitation enabled the remains of the British force to scramble to safety. Having gained a little time, Lawrence turned over the command to Colonel Inglis of the 32nd – something he should have done long before – and rode

The Residency in the
early days of the
siege of Lucknow.

back at full speed to Lucknow, realising that the defeat meant an
immediate attack on the Residency position.

History has dealt kindly with Henry Lawrence because he was
such a well-loved figure, but Chinhut was a disaster that should
never have occurred, and if it had not the siege of the Residency
might never have begun. On the field he had left half his best regiment, the 32nd Foot, together with some of the most competent of
his garrison's officers and NCOs. In addition to five guns and the
howitzer, he had lost 293 invaluable men with another 78 wounded
or overcome by the heat. With civilian volunteers, his force for the
defence of the Residency now consisted of only 1,720 able-bodied
men, and the survivors of Chinhut only managed to struggle back
because of the loyalty of Indian sepoys and because they were aided
by Indian women along the road who gave them water and milk.
The Hon Julia Inglis, wife of the colonel of the 32nd, who watched,
shocked, as they returned, wrote, 'You may imagine our feelings of
anxiety and consternation.' Other women turned more confidently
to prayers and the reading of the Bible, feeling they were 'in the
hands of the God of battles, and that without His will not all the
fury of the enemy could harm them.'

Fortunately, the rebels were as surprised by the victory of
Chinhut as Lawrence and made no attempt to take advantage of
the confusion by following up their victory with an immediate
attack on the Residency. Nevertheless, that prestige with which
Lawrence had held firm the population of Lucknow was now
shattered and, with the Europeans low in spirit, the mutineers
became increasingly bold as they followed his force through the
dusty alleys of the city. It was obvious now that the fortress of

Machchi Bewan, which overlooked and overawed the native area of Lucknow, would have to be abandoned because of the shortage of men, and that night, with a roar that shook the city, the fort was blown up together with 240 barrels of gunpowder and 5 million rounds of ammunition which might well have helped the defenders of the Residency. The garrison was brought in to swell the force available for the defence of the perimeter.

Amid the confusion and the clamour of the men arriving, Lawrence wrote a desperate letter to Havelock. 'Unless we are relieved quickly,' he said, 'say in fifteen or twenty days, we shall hardly be able to maintain our position.' It was a terrifying situation. Like so many others – Wheeler in Cawnpore, Havelock heading north, the troops at Delhi – he had only incomplete news of what was happening elsewhere in India. Isolated by events, a curtain of ignorance blotted out for him the rest of the vast territory between Calcutta and the Punjab. Occasional messages had emerged from a few of the larger places but concerning scores of smaller stations not a word of information was available. And what he said of his own position appeared to be correct. The fortifications which had been thrown up were still incomplete and the houses just outside had already been occupied by rebels, much to the disgust of Colonel Inglis, who had wished to destroy them. With true Victorian piety, Lawrence had allowed himself to be convinced that mosques and temples would not be fortified and had all along insisted that holy places and private property must be spared. As Inglis said later, they 'suffered severely from . . . tenderness to the religious prejudices and respect for the rights of . . . rebellious citizens and soldiery.'

As the rebels began to take up their positions, the defence was still in a state of chaos after Chinhut and the loss of the Machchi Bewan, and as new barricades were thrown up and guns were dragged into position, hundreds of the coolies who had been expected to do the manual work vanished into the city, taking their tools and stores with them. As mothers hastily sought safe places to shelter their children from the coming bombardment, beyond the defences, the mob, egged on by the mutinous sepoys, the dispossessed landowners and discontented Indian nobles, and the merchants who had been ruined by British policies, began to pour in a fire from the tops of the houses overlooking the position. Artillery fire followed, from guns and captured British howitzers, and on the second evening of the siege, 2 July, a shell from one of these struck the Residency. Lawrence was in his private apartment on the second floor, at the time, stretched exhausted on his bed.

While Wilson, his aide, begged him to go below, he had continued to dictate orders, accompanied by his nephew, George, and a coolie working the punkah, and just as Wilson read the instructions back to him, the shell smashed through the roof. Blinded by the flash, deafened by the crash and choking on the smoke and dust, Wilson staggered to his feet in the darkness, to hear Lawrence's voice calling feebly, 'I am killed.' The coolie had had his foot torn off, young Lawrence's shirt had been blown from his back, while Lawrence himself, still on the bed, lay in a pool of blood. It was already clear he was dying. His left thigh was torn open but the pelvis was also smashed and there was no chance of amputation. When he asked how long he had to live, the doctor told him at first 'Many hours yet, sir', but he later admitted that he had no more than 48 hours of life left to him. In extreme agony, still endeavouring to dictate orders for the defence, he died on the 4th and was buried in a communal plot. The pallbearers, privates of the 32nd, bent to kiss the cold face before he was lowered into the grave.

The plight of the Lucknow garrison was well known to Havelock. Lawrence's messages had reached him at Cawnpore where he was trying to reorganise his small force and give it the opportunity to recover from exhaustion and disease. Rigid in his sense of duty, when looting started, he ordered the provost-marshal 'to hang up, in their uniform, all British soldiers that plunder', and set about collecting boats to enable him to cross the river. On 20 July, by which time the 'fifteen or twenty days' that Lawrence had hoped the garrison at Lucknow could hold out had already expired, reinforcements arrived by steamer from Allahabad, and Neill arrived by road with more.

By this time, Havelock had heard of Lawrence's death but he was still in no position to move. He had to leave a force behind him to hold Cawnpore or he, too, would be cut off from help as the Nana Sahib returned. He chose a defensive site close to the ferry across the Ganges and, on a small raised plateau where his force could command both the river banks and the surrounding countryside, an earthwork was constructed by Mowbray Thompson, one of the four survivors of the Nana Sahib's massacre at the boats. Into it Havelock placed three hundred men under the command of Neill, who was thus left to devise his incredible tortures for the men he had captured.

Despite the condition of his men, Havelock determined to move

ahead to Lucknow. His force was tiny – minute compared with the numbers of the rebels he was expecting to face – but again and again in almost all the campaigns until the end of the Mutiny there was this same astonishing difference between the British forces and the enemy, and the same indifference to the odds on the part of the commanders. Even crossing the river presented problems for Havelock, because all the native boatmen had fled. But, with a promise of an amnesty, he persuaded them to return and, with 20 boats and the steamer which had brought reinforcements from Allahabad, he began to get his men across the mile-wide, swift-running stream. Hampered by the monsoon rains, it was not until five days later, however, that he was able to move off with his 1,500 men and ten guns. Pausing at Mangalwar, five miles along the road to Lucknow, to allow his transport and supplies to come up, he wrote, in reply to a telegram from Canning, that the chances of relieving Lucknow were 'hourly multiplying'. He had received a plan of the city and information from spies and messages from Inglis containing phrases written in Greek to confuse the mutineers if captured.

The remains of the Machchi Bewan.

On 29 July, he moved off towards Unao where the rebels were strongly positioned with a swamp on their right and their main force behind a fortified village. Forced into a direct attack by the swamp on one side and the flooded countryside on the other, he

drove the enemy back, capturing their guns. But even as his men drew breath, he learned that six thousand more rebels were heading from Lucknow for Unao and it was imperative that he got there first. Pushing through the town, he took up a position similar to the one he had just captured, commanding the road and surrounded by swamps. Not knowing he was there, the advancing rebels marched straight on to his guns and, as they attempted to form battle order, their artillery sank in the marshes and they fled, leaving behind 300 dead and 15 guns.

The fighting was still not over. After a short rest Havelock pushed on to Bashiratganj, a walled town six miles further along the road. The rebels were entrenched in front of it in an impregnable position so Havelock made no attempt to attack but simply by-passed it and forced them to flee.

With three victories under their belts in one day, the British were cock-a-hoop, but their position was dangerous as they threw themselves down to rest. The force was now down to only 850 men, 88 killed and wounded having been lost, as well as all the men who had collapsed through heat, exhaustion or cholera. With only a few more casualties, it would be impossible to advance any further, especially since a third of the artillery ammunition was gone and Havelock was only a third of the way to Lucknow. With heavy concentrations of rebels across his path and faced with the likelihood of arriving at his destination without the means to defend himself, let alone relieve the garrison, he was forced to let the victories he had won slip away and return to Mangalwar.

Meanwhile in Lucknow, Colonel Inglis had divided the command and, taking over the military side of the defence himself, had given the civil side to another soldier, Major Banks, rather than to the unbalanced and hot-headed Martin Gubbins. The garrison was now beginning to look with anxiety towards the south, their heads cocked for the sound of Havelock's guns. Already all the male civilians had offered themselves to Inglis, to serve with the ordinary privates of the 32nd, and, exhausted, forgetting what it was like to sleep in a bed, tortured by lice – which the women delicately called 'light infantry' – they did twenty hours duty a day and more, some of it in pouring rain, standing guard or doing the sort of heavy manual work for which they had previously hired coolies. With 25 heavy guns commanding the position, some only a few hundred yards away, it was all done under a continuous galling fire and by 22 July, even before Havelock had crossed the Ganges, the top storey of the Residency building had become untenable. The lower half was occupied by soldiers while the banqueting hall a short distance away, where a hospital had been organised, was in a similar state and sick and wounded crowded the ground floor.

Conditions had deteriorated rapidly, yet one or two people, because they had been farsighted and possessed funds, still managed to maintain their old standards. As Russell, the correspondent of *The Times*, later discovered, 'whilst some were starving . . . others were living on the good things of the land . . .' and caste was as strong among the English as it was among the Indians. 'There was a good deal of etiquette about visiting and speaking,' Russell wrote. '. . . Strange, whilst cannon shot and shell were rending the walls about their ears, whilst disease was knocking at the door of every room, that those artificial rules of life still exercised their force; that petty jealousy and "caste" reigned in the Residency; the "upper ten" with stoical grandeur would die the "upper ten" . . . It is a pity that our admiration for the heroism of that glorious defence should be marred by such stories as these.'

For the less well-heeled, the junior officers and rankers, life was much more difficult. One officer, whose clothes had been reduced to rags in his flight to the city, was wearing a uniform made out of the Residency billiard table cloth, and the women, often living in squalor in damp cellars and possessing nothing in the way of comfort, were little better off. With their hordes of servants, most of them had never had to cook in their lives and had never learned how, and now it was difficult for them even to get their food heated, while, when it was placed on the table, it was immediately covered by flies which swarmed over it, black and shining and loathsome. Windows were barricaded with bookcases but stray bullets and cannon balls continued to pick off unsuspecting people. Fortu- 117 nately the rebels were short of ammunition and pieces of wood, iron, copper, coins, even bullocks' horns, were being fired into the defences. But even these managed to kill, and rats and mice plagued the women as they huddled in the cellars during the alarms, clutching their children and in some nervous cases phials of prussic acid in case the besiegers broke in. There was talk at one time of blowing them up if it came to the worst.

With the people from the outposts packed into the defensive perimeter, every house was desperately overcrowded now and cholera and smallpox cases could not be segregated. Already the wounded were in a terrible condition, among them Dr Brydon, the sole survivor of the Kabul disaster fifteen years before, who was now enduring his second siege. The injured lay on couches, covered with blood and often with vermin, attended by the women who were hampered by the absence of bandages and even of soap. Food consisted of ground corn, shreds of beef, biscuits and rice, and several suicides took place.

Only the fact that the mutineers could not agree among themselves over their leaders and finally entrusted the command to courtiers of the ex-king rather than to officers with experience of fighting had prevented a large-scale assault, but on 19 July a determined attempt was finally made. A mine was exploded under the fortifications – fortunately without much effect – and the rebels rushed to the attack. Although their leader managed to plant a green standard on the parapet, the defenders threw them back, chiefly because the mutineers, although willing to brave the bullets, were not prepared to face the bayonets that waited them. Four of the garrison were killed and 12 wounded, but while the besiegers lost a lot of their enthusiasm, the besieged drew new heart from the event and gained a great deal of confidence from the victory and the belief that by now Havelock could not possibly be very far away.

Havelock, however, was still at Mangalwar and unable to move. He had found a good defensive position which was easily supplied from Cawnpore, and from here he had sent back to Neill saying he must wait for another battery and another thousand men before he could push on. Neill, an impulsive, sometimes unbalanced man, tried with an urgent abusive letter to force him to advance, and Havelock came down on him like a thunderbolt. He had already suffered considerably from Neill's dislike and he told him bluntly that he would have no further attempts to dictate his actions.

He continued to wait in an agony of impatience because he had learned that he could expect nothing for several weeks, owing to the fact that the sepoys at Dinapur – in a position to threaten any attempt to send reinforcements up the Grand Trunk Road – had mutinied as a result of inept handling, and it was important that the reinforcements he needed should first re-establish control of the area. Only 257 men were available for him, not even enough to make up his casualties. The position seemed hopeless but, despite the absence of help, Havelock, aware of the plight of Lucknow, set off again on 4 August, only to learn that the rebels were back again at Bashiratganj. Once more he defeated them by outflanking their positions, but again, due to his lack of cavalry, he was unable to stop them escaping with their guns.

Without adequate maps, all of which had been lost in the sack of Cawnpore, he only knew that they were now established at Nawabganj and that a bridge at Sai which he needed had been destroyed, and the crossing was defended by 30,000 rebels. He had also heard of the mutiny at Gwalior and that the men of the Gwalior contingent were threatening to endanger Cawnpore and the communications with Allahabad, while the rebels from Dinapur were supposed to be advancing into Oudh. With the expectation that a third of his force would become casualties as he fought his way to Lucknow, leaving him only 700 men – and this not allowing for casualties from disease and exhaustion – he would have only a tiny force to drive through the narrow alleys of Lucknow to the Residency. After a consultation with his staff, he was once more obliged to retire to Mangalwar.

With no sign of Havelock, by the beginning of August it was becoming clear to the defenders of Lucknow that the rations must be cut, and they were using their ingenuity to provide substitutes for the things they lacked. Already the place stank from the dead rotting in their shallow graves and the mules and bullocks dissolving into putrefaction because there was no one to bury them or burn them. Desperate for news, the one thing that sustained them was the tenuous contact with Havelock by means of messages carried out by loyal Indians who received what were to them fabulous sums for their risks. Inglis wrote that the rebels had pushed up to the walls of the defences and begged Havelock to hurry, but the messenger brought back nothing but promises. Help would come as soon as possible, they were told.

Every night the sky beyond the trees was watched for the rockets Havelock had promised to send up as a signal of his arrival and all day heads were cocked for the sound of his guns. His messages – 'You must aid us in every way, even to cutting your way out' – seemed to indicate he was out of touch with the situation and Inglis wrote back irritatedly: 'I have upwards of 120 sick and wounded, and at least 220 women and 130 children and no carriage of any description.' On 28 August, the messenger brought back Havelock's reply, saying that he expected reinforcements in between 20 to 25 days. 'I can only say,' he wrote, 'do not negotiate, but rather perish sword in hand.' It shocked the defenders. Already they had defended their position for sixty days and it seemed incredible that Havelock could not cover the last 53 miles to their relief.

But a move by Havelock from Mangalwar had become impossible by this time. Gloomy now, depressed by the constant waiting, his men camping out in drenching rain on flooded ground, he could only establish himself more firmly, knowing that so long as he remained stubbornly where he was in Oudh, his presence meant that he had to be constantly watched by a large force of rebels who would otherwise have swelled the force besieging Lucknow.

A panic cry from Neill in Cawnpore that he was threatened by 4,000 men and five guns finally decided him to retreat. If Cawnpore were lost again it would be impossible for reinforcements to come by river, and he had already started back across the river when his scouts reported that the rebels were again in large numbers at Bashiratganj. With such a force in his rear, a crossing of the river would invite attack and, accordingly, in heavy rain he once again marched on Unao and for a third time prepared an attack on Bashiratganj. Forced this time into a frontal attack, the 78th Highlanders were sent against the enemy guns under heavy fire. Capturing them, they turned them on the rebel infantry behind and drove them away in a rout. After chasing them through the town, Havelock again could do no more than return to Mangalwar and cross the river on the 13th, still in pouring rain, destroying the bridges behind him.

With cholera rampant, he realised he would not have a single man left if he did not rest his force. With 4,000 rebels collecting at Bithur, however, though his own force was reduced to 335 fit men, he decided he must attack them. He left only 100 men with Neill at Cawnpore and moved off on the night of 15 August. By the time he arrived in position, his men had been moving all day in a blinding heat and he had lost many of them through sunstroke. The rebels lay behind plantations of sugar cane and castor oil plants, interspersed with villages, and, with a swollen stream in front of them, the only access to the town was via a small stone bridge.

Though the rebel infantry was routed, their guns did a great deal of damage before they were driven off at the point of the bayonet. Once again the lack of cavalry prevented pursuit. The following day, hearing that the rebels had moved towards Cawnpore and

Opposite
Major C. J. S. Crough, 5th Bengal European Cavalry, winning the V.C., 15 August 1857.

120

The flight from
Lucknow, 1858. From
the painting by
Abraham Solomon.

were now threatening Neill's weak garrison, Havelock again moved back to Cawnpore, less 72 killed, wounded and sick. He knew full well this time that he could not do anything more for Lucknow.

His campaign, though brilliant and courageous, had, in fact, done a great deal of harm, and his return across the river encouraged local chieftains and landowners in Oudh who had not so far joined the rebellion to add their support. Even his victories were interpreted by the rebels as failures because of his inability to follow them up and break through to Lucknow. Though they had been defeated in battle again and again, the bulk of their forces had always escaped so that Havelock's little army had been frittered away for nothing. The military uprising changed its face as the whole province rose in arms.

Although Havelock became a national hero in England, it is possible that he was judged as much as anything by his standards of Victorian piety, and when Russell of *The Times* arrived, he noticed his reputation was not so great in India as he had expected. 'What a silence about Havelock!' he wrote. 'As we approach the soil to which he and his soldiers had given a European interest, the splendour of his reputation diminished.'

Chapter 8

The Storming of Delhi

To the north, at Delhi, the British still grimly hung on, staring down on to the vast walls and bastions of the city and impatiently awaiting the reinforcements that were necessary to make any assault on the place successful. With the constant fighting – the sallies to destroy enemy batteries and the rebel attacks on British posts – in one week 25 officers and 400 men had been killed or wounded and, though the little army had increased to 6,600, the drain from casualties and the diseases that were always with them completely destroyed the value of reinforcements.

Their only consolation was that behind them the first steps had been taken to bring the disturbed area of Central India under control. Durand had at last been able to move on Mhow which was reoccupied on 1 August, and now, apart from isolated outbreaks, the area was quiet and it seemed possible to send a few men to Delhi. A mobile column of 4,200 men under the command of thirty-four-year-old John Nicholson, now created brigadier, was also moving down from Lahore, while a siege train was being prepared to follow. A strong, dark, unsmiling man, John Nicholson was energetic, courageous and imaginative and, like Hodson, belonged in spirit to the previous century. Though most of his service in India had been as a political officer, he had a tremendous reputation in the Punjab and he did not wait for the slow-moving column he led but rode ahead of it to Delhi.

He arrived on 7 August. He had been indifferent to discomfort and when his officers had begged for a halt in the heat of the day he had granted it but had remained himself bolt upright in the burning sun, waiting impatiently until his men had recovered. En route he had disarmed regiments at Phillaur and Jullundur, and with news of an uprising at Sialkot and the bayoneting of men, women and children and the advance of the mutineers to Gurdaspur to stir up mutiny there, he had commandeered pony carts and bullock carts and got his force there before them. Allowing the rebels to walk into the trap he had set, he had driven them into the River Ravi where the survivors took refuge on an island in midstream. As the column had moved on to Delhi, with officers wearing foliage in their hats or constructing awnings of leaves over the carts and gun carriages to keep off the merciless sun, men and horses had succumbed to the heat. Impervious himself, Nicholson had driven his force on, however, sweeping in men and batteries as he went, to the indignation of commanding officers.

Regarded by his detractors as a bully and by his admirers as a

Opposite
The blowing in of the Kashmir Gate, 14 September 1857.

125

John Nicholson.

hero, if nothing else Nicholson – or Nickal Seyn, as he was known to
his troops – was an intelligent, brave man. He had long been expecting trouble in India. 'For years,' he had said, 'I have watched
the army and felt sure they only wanted their opportunity to try
their strength with us.' Now that they had tried, he was in no two
minds what to do about it. Religious with the fire of a Scottish
covenanter, he had no time for gentle methods. 'Mutiny is like
small-pox,' he claimed. 'It spreads quickly and must be crushed as
soon as possible.' When sepoys had risen at Naushera near Peshawar, it had been Nicholson who had persuaded the brigadier-
general in command of the district, Sir Sidney Cotton, to disarm
his own troops. The air had immediately cleared, he said, 'as if by a
thunderstorm' and the chieftains around, who had been waiting
to see which way the wind would blow, had at once declared for
126   the British, so that friends were suddenly 'as thick as summer flies'.

The mutinous sepoys were then rounded up and forty of them were blown from guns.

Nicholson loathed the mutineers and felt that flaying alive, impalement and burning were barely good enough for the murderers of women and children, and his reputation was so great that immediately he arrived outside Delhi, everyone expected the situation to improve. He was not known personally to many in the camp but it was not long before he was visiting the outposts and inspecting the lines to get the feel of the place. He was a tall man of commanding presence with the ruthlessness that makes a man great, though his dourness often acted as a damper on the spirits of other men.

Strictly speaking, he had no official position at Delhi. His appointment was unauthorised by Royal Warrant and his arrogance irritated the Queen's officers, but everyone was nevertheless aware that he was the man for the job. When his column had arrived the numbers of the Delhi Field Force had doubled, but the force inside the city had also grown in size and when the heavy siege train of over 600 bullock carts, labouring heavily over the rain-sodden roads, approached, the mutineers heard about it and marched out to intercept it. Nicholson led 2,500 men and sixteen guns against them through a torrential rainstorm. The roads were appalling and as they made their way across swampy ground, the guns kept sinking. But, with Sir Theophilus Metcalfe, the Delhi magistrate, acting as guide, they were brought within five miles of the enemy outposts near the town of Najafgarh.

As the mutineers' guns shelled the attacking force, the infantry was ordered to lie down to allow their own guns to reply, then

Guns captured by Nicholson at Najafgarh being brought into the British camp in Delhi.

Nicholson led them across a sea of mud against the enemy strong-point in an old *serai* or travellers' rest house. For the British the battle was almost bloodless and, with 13 captured guns, the force, despite the absence of food and shelter, felt it had done well, while the mutineers at Delhi were shocked by their first defeat since Badli-ke-serai in June.

The time for an attempt on the city was clearly ripe. The streets were unswept and as garbage piled up the smells and flies were as bad as on the Ridge, while the air was full of accusations and re-criminations. The king's sons were charged with embezzlement and indifference, and roisterings as wild as the drunken sepoys'; the troops were unpaid and hungry; and old scores were being settled by false denunciations that led to torture and death. News had also reached the British of considerable anxiety in the city, from which a messenger was even sent out in the hope of coming to terms. With the British suddenly cock-a-hoop after Nicholson's victory he was sent back with no doubt about the future.

He was not given a 'single promise of even bare life for anyone, from the king downwards.' Although there were 2,500 sick in the camp on the Ridge, 1,100 of them Europeans, there was a new feeling of expectation in the air.

Despite the arrival of the siege train on 4 September, great guns drawn by elephants and accompanied by their vast train of carts containing ammunition, Archdale Wilson's old habit of doubt was still heavy on him. He had done wonders about the camp, getting the loathsome carcasses of camels and elephants cleared and bring-ing order to duties and into the methods of fighting, so that there were no more of the foolhardy rushes after the enemy when they appeared which had cost so many lives. But, dispirited after an attack of dysentery, he considered his force far too small to move to the attack. The consequences of failure would have been terrible, he knew, and, unwilling to take the risk of a countrywide uprising that would follow an unsuccessful assault, he showed to Baird Smith a letter to the Governor-General containing his views.

Baird Smith had also made a great difference since his arrival. Waiting impatiently for the great siege guns, he had removed dangers which the ineptitude of his predecessor had allowed to remain, and had cleared thickets and hacked down trees, walls and buildings from where the rebel sharpshooters had sniped at the British. He had also built breastworks to give shelter and barricaded

The mutineers made ferocious sorties on the British posts throughout the siege of Delhi.

roads so that the charges by rebel cavalry which had so often troubled them in the past were halted. A driving, intelligent man, he read Wilson's letter angrily, furious at his hesitation. He was all for attack and he was undoubtedly right.

With the siege guns that had arrived he could now bring fire to bear on the rebel defences and the wait had gone on far too long. It was doing no good to British morale and, in the city, Bakht Khan, an artillery subadar who had been appointed commander-in-chief to the rebels, was not entirely trusted. Despite his stringent orders, he still found it hard to control the rebels, and the king could not control them at all. Their assaults towards the Ridge were tremendous teeming advances which left hundreds dead, and the wounded, since they had no surgeons, entirely without aid. Yet, despite the lack of organisation, they continued to make ferocious sorties through the drenching rainstorms, catching unwary British outposts unprepared and driving them in, to control the approaches to the Ridge for a dangerous half-hour or so until the British managed to recover their wits and force them back through the dripping trees to the city.

Nevertheless, they were beginning to grow worried now. Despite everything they had done, the British were still there outside the city, grim-faced, patient and enduring, living all the time with unspeakable things which would have shocked them in England but at Delhi no longer even touched the heart, and as an indication of how Delhi itself felt, merchants had even begun to leave the city streets for the camp on the Ridge, to arrive through the steaming puddles with goods to sell. As Baird Smith, sick and limping from

129

As native troops joined the Delhi Field Force there were twenty Indians to every white man.

a neglected wound, had dourly guessed, if they were resolute and imaginative, they now stood a good chance of capturing the place. The Delhi Field Force had grown again with reinforcements, though there were still twenty Indians to every white man – Gurkhas, Pathans, Muslims, Sikhs, and all the untiring lowly servants who carried food or water or the dhoolies for the sick and injured – and patience was beginning to change to impatience.

Wilson continued to hesitate, however, until Baird Smith had had as much of him as he could stand. 'The simple truth is,' he wrote, 'that I had such contempt for Wilson's military capacity and found him throughout the siege operations so uniformly obstructive by his dread of responsibility and his moral timidity that I saw as little about him as I could. . . . I believe his mind to have been off its usual balance . . . and he was literally more difficult to deal with than the enemy.'

Whenever Baird Smith's home truths were offered Wilson sulked and complained too much was being asked of him. 'I have already more than I can manage,' he wrote back, 'and my head gets into such a state that I feel nearly mad sometimes.' Baird Smith was unrelenting. 'I am satisfied Wilson has gone off his head,' he said finally in disgust, while Nicholson was equally unsympathetic. 'Wilson's head is going,' he reported coldly. 'He says so himself, and it is quite evident he speaks the truth.'

130

Baird Smith's view, like that of all the young and energetic men, had all along been a simple one. Risks not faced would simply grow, while Nicholson considered that, with the game now in their hands, they only wanted 'a player to move the pieces'. The arguments were sound. The army was still riddled with cholera – so that it was dreadful 'to see the agony and hear the groans of the men' – and the monsoon, always an unhealthy season, with the rain falling in torrents for 24 hours at a time to cover clothes with mildew and turn the ground to a steaming quagmire, had increased the sickness. The atmosphere was hot and stifling, and a stench of death hung over the hospital area. There were no women nurses despite Florence Nightingale's offer to bring out a party, and the flies crawled in swarms over the heads of the sick and wounded, into their ears and nostrils – even, the Rev. John Rotton found, into his mouth as he read to or prayed with the dying. The Bible he used, stained by fly marks, reminded him to the end of his life of the hours he had spent in those terrible surroundings. Food was covered by them and even a cup of tea became a mass of drowning black insects the minute it was poured.

John Lawrence was still taking the northern frontier on trust, and sending every man he could muster. Afghan troops had arrived from Kabul but they were considered to be spies for Dost Mohammed, their Emir, who was eager to hear of the condition of the British, and it was noticed that though they 'made a great display' they were never involved in the fighting. Kashmir troops arrived on 7 September, the first indication of their arrival the sound of discordant music that brought the German bandmaster of the 61st to his feet. 'Vot is dat?' he said. 'No regiment in camp can play such vile music.' They arrived playing an English air, drums beating, colours flying, Sikhs and hillmen of good appearance, their ludicrous style of marching and their strange, outlandish uniforms and the shrill discord of their bands creating great amusement.

Faced with these increases in his force and constantly badgered by Baird Smith and Nicholson, Wilson finally gave way. He still held that the chances of success were 'anything but favourable', however, and in a note pencilled on Baird Smith's memorandum, he made it quite clear that while he had agreed to an assault, he felt he had been forced into it and had no wish to be held responsible in the case of failure.

It was fortunate he *had* agreed because, according to Field Marshal Lord Roberts, then simply Lieutenant Fred Roberts, Nicholson was talking very strongly of taking the unusual step of superseding him, whether he liked it or not. With Chamberlain wounded

The native troops
included hillmen of
outlandish appearance.

and with Wilson removed, Nicholson would have been the next senior officer, but he had no wish for it to be said that he had plotted Wilson's supercession simply to get the chief command himself and he was proposing that it should be given instead to Colonel George Campbell, of the 52nd Foot – though it seemed clear he intended to be the power behind the throne. He and Baird Smith were aware that in any assault there would be heavy casualties but the desperate situation of the Mutiny called for desperate measures. A quick success now, however bloody, would indicate that the cause of the rebels could not be sustained and would draw hesitant chieftains to the British side all over India.

As the stifling days continued, fraying the nerves of both sides, the plan for the attack was drawn up by Baird Smith and another engineer officer, Alexander Taylor. Every detail was carefully covered and their intention was to breach the walls with batteries and mines. It was decided that the section of the city to be attacked should be that facing the British cantonments and near to the banks of the river, where there was good cover for the engineers.

All the necessities of an assault – gabions, fascines and scaling ladders – had already been made and on the evening of 7 September, despite fire from the city and Wilson's apparent inclination to withdraw them again, the first battery of heavy guns was placed in position. By the following afternoon, the Mori Bastion guarding the Kabul Gate had been smashed. A second battery was moved up at once and by the 11th this was hammering away at the walls nearer to the river. In blinding heat and under heavy fire which knocked over man after man, a third battery was soon also in action from a dangerously close position and the walls of Delhi began to crumble before the gaze of the British in cascades of falling stone and swirling dust.

The attack was to be made on 14 September and a reconnaissance on the night of the 13th indicated that the breaches the guns had made were large enough. There were to be five columns but none of them was strong because numbers had been reduced by casualties during the siting of the batteries. Three of the columns, under Nicholson, were to attack the area of the Kashmir Gate and a fourth under Major Reid was to capture the suburb of Kishanganj outside the walls, to cover the right flank and then attack the Kabul Gate on the east of the city which would be opened by Nicholson's men. The fifth column under Brigadier Longfield, was to constitute the reserve, while the cavalry brigade, under Hope Grant, would cover the camp on the Ridge against attack. It was a desperate plan. The tiny assault force was about to attempt to capture a great, fortified city full of rebellious soldiers. Nicholson was gambling on the mutineers being divided among themselves. He was fully aware that this time there must be no mistake, because a message had been received that John Lawrence could not guarantee the Punjab for more than a day or two longer.

During the hours of darkness, officers and men prepared by lamplight for the morning. They donned clean clothing against infection in case of wounds, carefully loaded their pistols, filled their flasks and water bottles, and – to protect their heads in those days before steel helmets – wound puggris or turbans round their forage caps. Then, writing last letters home or reading their Bibles or making their wills, they settled themselves to rest. It was hard to sleep, however, because nervous officers continued to talk in low tones or fiddle with their weapons. The men were fallen in at midnight and their orders read to them. Because of the need for speed, no one was to go to the aid of the wounded. If the attack were successful they would be collected later. If not, then they would be no worse off than the unwounded. There was to be no plundering and there were to be no prisoners – less because of the desire for vengeance than because there were not sufficient men to guard them – but women and children were to be spared.

The ditch in front of the walls was to be crossed by scaling ladders, after which the individual commanders would make the decision, according to the circumstances they faced, whether to penetrate into the teeming alleys of the city or to make for the palace. It was Nicholson's belief that the mutineers would not stand up to a determined attack and he gave instructions that, to save British lives, they were not to be pressed too hard but given the chance to retire.

After a prayer, the 5,000 troops involved began to take up their positions. With the air alive with explosions and thick with smoke, flying stones and dust, the guns hammered away in the dark at the breaches. Because the mutineers had effected repairs during the night, these had to be opened again, and the sun was already high in the brassy sky when the order for the attack came. With Nicholson leading, the 60th Rifles swept forward, yelling and cheering, the second column following in close support. Despite a hail of fire that kicked up the flayed earth, the first breach was captured. The second column captured the second breach and, as the mutineers retreated, the British began to pour into the city near the Kashmir Gate and drive between the mud walls of the narrow streets in a yelling press of men, drunk on a kind of fighting madness.

As the two columns had advanced, hacking and stabbing at the sepoys, a party of British and Indian sappers with gun-powder and sandbags, under Lieutenants Home and Salkeld, had made for the gate itself. With them was a bugler to sound the Advance as soon as the gate had been blown. Man after man was shot down to fall among the bodies and the rubbish in the ditch but the powder was placed in position and the portfire applied. With the man who had applied it diving frantically for the ditch, the gate went up in a chaos of dust and flying timbers and stones. The blare of the bugle went unheard in the din but Colonel Campbell, in command of the third column, heard the explosion and led his men forward through the smoke. Only three planks were left of the draw-bridge and the breach was so narrow only one man at a time could squeeze through the littered debris. The third column did not hesitate, however, and pushed through to join those men of the first column who had scrambled through the bastion. Apart from the dead, the square behind had emptied of rebels and two thousand men had forced their way into the city.

The first column, under Nicholson, and the second under Colonel William Jones, of the 61st (Queen's) Foot, should now have captured the Kabul Gate to let in the fourth column, while Campbell's third column made for the Jama Masjid, a mosque which held roughly 'the same rank in India that St Peter's did in the Roman

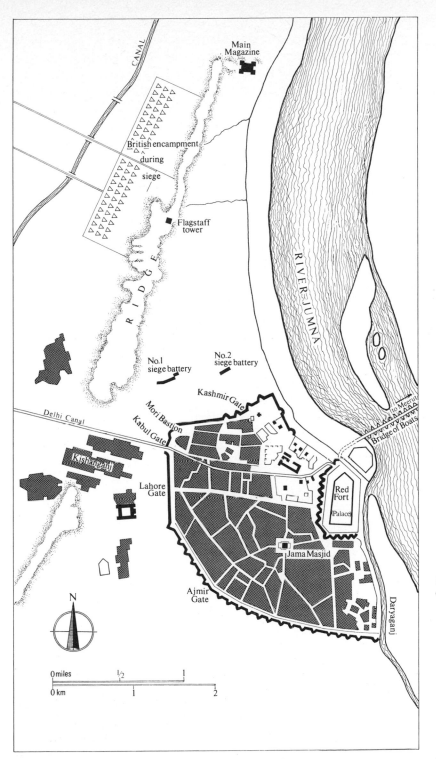

CANAL

Main
Magazine

British encampment

during

siege

Flagstaff
tower

R I D G E

RIVER JUMNA

No.1
siege battery

No.2
siege battery

Kashmir Gate

Mori Bastion

Delhi Canal

Kabul Gate

to Meerut

Bridge of Boats

Kishanganj

Lahore
Gate

Red
Fort

(Palace)

Ajmir
Gate

Jama Masjid

Daryaganj

N

0 miles   ½   1
0 km   1   2

Delhi at the time
of the Mutiny.

Catholic world.' Jones, however, had lost his bearings in the narrow, smoke-filled alleys and there was only confusion. With sepoys on roofs and walls knocking them over like ninepins, his men could only just hold their ground.

Meanwhile, Major Reid, leading the fourth column, had found his guns had not come up and, with the mutineers well established in front of Kishanganj, he could not clear them from his path. He was opposed by some 15,000 well-trained men in a good position – if he should fail – to attack either the camp on the Ridge or the flanks of the other columns. Men were already dropping under their fire and as Reid fell wounded in the head, confusion reigned. Although the senior officer was Captain Richard Lawrence, in command of a body of untrained men from Kashmir, Captain Muter, of the 60th, regarded him merely as a political officer and issued conflicting orders. Driven back, the Kashmiris broke in disorder and for a while it seemed that the rebels might push through the gap they had left. They were stopped just in time by shrapnel, and Hope Grant, seeing what had happened, moved up the cavalry. For two hours under a heavy fire from the walls, the cavalrymen sat their horses in line, constantly moving their position to clear the plunging animals that had been brought down. They held the position until reinforced.

By this time, however, the second column, at the Kabul Gate, finding itself unsupported, had been halted. Feeling he had overshot his target, Jones was hesitant despite the high spirit of his junior officers and men who, after the first bloody victory as they had entered the city, were ready for anything. But many of the enemy, freed by Reid's failure, had now returned to the city and were holding them down with a heavy fire from houses near the walls, and for a while there was a great danger even that their high spirits would break in panic.

In a towering rage, aware that everything was in danger of going wrong, Nicholson ordered Campbell, who had broken through the Kashmir Gate, to press on to the Jama Masjid and reformed his own column at the Kabul Gate and pushed on towards the Lahore Gate opposite Kishanganj. To reach it, a strongpoint known as the Burn Bastion had to be passed and, to get at it, it was necessary to press through stifling narrow lanes covered by heavy fire from houses on either side.

Nicholson was well aware that it was important to recover the initiative lost by Reid's failure and he flung the 1st Fusiliers forward, only to see the panting, exhausted men forced back by the fire of grapeshot and musketry and showers of stones. Reforming,

The storming of
the Kashmir Gate.

they again attacked, stumbling over the bodies of friends, the
squirming shapes of the wounded and all the bloody litter of battle
strewn about the street. The gun that held them up was captured
but, as they made for a second gun beyond it, they were again
forced to withdraw. Seeing his whole plan in danger of failing,
Nicholson sprang forward to lead them in another desperate attack.
As he raised his tulwar and stepped forward, shouting scornful en-
couragement, the thud of a bullet striking his left side under his
arm was heard even above the din of battle.

'You are hit, sir,' someone said, and Nicholson irritatedly replied 'Yes, yes', and sank slowly to his knees, grinding his teeth with
rage and frustration. As he fell, the officers with him decided to
retire. Their casualties seemed enormous and they were shaken by
the cost of the assault.

Campbell, meanwhile, had headed across the city for the Jama
Masjid but the mosque was sandbagged and its arches bricked up
so that without sappers and gunpowder he was helpless against it.
Under heavy fire, he retired to await assistance from the other
columns, but Nicholson's failure to reach the Lahore Gate had left   137

Subadar Bahadur, the last survivor of the attack on the Kashmir Gate.

him isolated and he fell back towards the Kashmir Gate and grimly established himself in a street leading into the heart of the city ready for a second attempt.

By the evening, the British had got themselves into a very difficult position. Although they were inside the city, their flank was threatened and casualties amounted to 1,170, many of them caused in the labyrinth of roofs, shaded courtyards and houses, where they had gone in search of loot. They were found days later, mutilated and with their throats cut. Not losing heart, however, the advanced

The 78th Highlanders
at Lucknow. The action
in which Private Henry
Ward won the V.C. for
remaining with the
dooly of Captain
Havelock.

positions were fortified and attempts were made to establish contact between them.

Hearing of the casualties and the mortal wounding of Nicholson, and out of touch with the assaulting force inside the narrow alleys of the city, Wilson was more than willing to cry 'Enough' and order a withdrawal. But Baird Smith and a few others realised that, in spite of the failures, they were on the brink of success and refused to allow him to do so. That night looting started, spreading into the next day. The area of the Kashmir Gate was occupied by merchants who sold European liquor and when the soldiers broke into the cellars they started an orgy of drunkenness. Too late, Wilson gave the order for the liquor stores to be destroyed. But the mutineers failed to take advantage of the chaos and the British were left alone throughout the whole of the 15th, the troops, many of them inflamed with drink, yelling and stumbling about the littered streets, smashing ancient treasures of which they had no understanding and bayoneting everyone they came across with a coloured skin. 'British soldiers must eat and they must drink,' Hope Grant wrote bitterly. 'Would to God they drank less.' Nevertheless individual men had distinguished themselves in the fury of combat. Private soldiers had been promoted sergeant on the spot for their gallantry and the surgeon of the 61st, finding the wounded he was tending in danger of attack, drew his sword and led a charge as a soldier.

On the 16th, rounding up the befuddled troops, the columns began to press forward again. The suburb of Kishanganj was evacuated by the rebels and the magazine captured with 171 guns and howitzers and a great deal of ammunition, but the street fighting was costly because every house was full of mutineers and every alley saw savage little battles in the smoke of burning buildings. They now began to shell the palace itself with artillery and, though the mutineers continued to resist, using groups of screaming women and children as shields, others were now beginning to stream out of the city across the bridge of boats. Another attack on the Lahore Gate was repulsed, however, because the British troops, still half-drunk, refused to follow their officers, but the Burn Bastion fell at last on the 19th and, early the following morning, Jones finally captured the Lahore Gate which allowed reinforcements to stream in. Dividing his force in two, he now sent one half to the Jama Masjid and set off himself with the other to the Ajmir Gate, the last great gate facing the British. The Jama Masjid fell without much difficulty and the commander of the detachment sent a message to Wilson – despite the successes, he was still bewailing his

Opposite The wounded at Lucknow, in which three members of the 78th Highlanders won the V.C. for bringing in the wounded to the Residency.

difficulties and his ill health – to make an attack on the palace at once.

The palace was occupied and with it the fort commanding the bridge of boats, but the king and his followers had left the previous day and all that was found were carriages, cannon and the plunder of the mutineers. There were still thousands of rebels concealed in the twisting alleys and narrow streets, however, and the British sought them out mercilessly and cut them down in a frenzy of hatred in hand-to-hand battles. The murder of Mary Clifford in the first days of the uprising had made her brother 'a changed being', Griffiths noticed. Clifford had heard that his sister had been raped then, naked, had been dragged up the main street behind a gun carriage and cut to pieces in the presence of the king's sons, and he had arrived to join in the assault, armed with a sword, revolver and rifle. Now Griffiths met him, covered with blood, his eyes wild, announcing that he had put to death everyone he had come across, 'not excepting women and children'.

The story of his sister, like that of the editor of *The Delhi Gazette* and his family being tortured and having their throats cut with broken glass, was not true, but no one bothered to question it, and other men, their wives and sisters and children murdered, similarly went berserk. The soldiers' appearance became inhuman. Hearts had hardened in the long wait and there was no mercy. Their eyes 'flashing with passion and revenge,' their faces wet with sweat and blackened with powder, it would have been useless, Griffiths knew, to attempt to check them.

The terrified old king and his court had taken refuge in the tomb of Humayun, one of the Moghul kings, six miles from Delhi and on the 20th, refusing to accompany the fleeing mutineers, he surrendered to Hodson on the promise of his life. He was taken back to the city and, on the following day, hearing that three of his sons – all of whom had been implicated in the worst of the atrocities against the British and were well capable of rallying the rebels because of their royal blood – were also in hiding there, Hodson returned to the tomb. Hoping for clemency but without any guarantee of safety, the three men surrendered and appeared in a small covered cart drawn by bullocks. The men of Hodson's Horse accompanied it on either side followed by a crowd of several thousand Muslims, sullenly watching the degradation of their leaders' surrender.

On edge, smoking cigars to keep his nerves steady, Hodson's second-in-command watched Hodson controlling the crowd. Then, claiming that it was safer to get rid of the three men rather than risk an attempt at rescue, Hodson forced them to strip – a shameful act

to an Indian – and, seizing a Colt revolver, he shot them dead one by one. Placing the muzzle of the weapon so close the flesh was singed, he left them where they fell so they could be seen by everyone. Hodson admitted he had enjoyed killing them and, though he did not expect his action to go uncriticised, with the uproar that was being raised everywhere about vengeance he certainly did not expect the chorus of protest that arose. Despite his reputation for unscrupulousness and lack of principle, Hodson's fame had grown out of all proportion to his rank but the murder of the princes did him great harm. Before long gossip was dragging up the old stories of the trouble he had had over money and he was being accused – not entirely unfairly – of storing away vast quantities of loot.

In fact, the princes' fate was sealed from the moment they surrendered. Hundreds were being despatched and it was only a question of whether they would die by a bullet or by the rope. Their deaths marked the end of the rebellion in Delhi. The troops were already tramping in their torn and filthy uniforms through the palace, even into the royal harem where the lingering scent of attar fought with the stink of death from the city, and Taylor, the man who had made the plan for the assault with Baird Smith, rode his horse up the steps in style. In a way, it was a hollow victory, though, because, as a salute of guns announced the end of resistance and the Union Jack was hoisted above the bastions, the captured city was only a smoking, charred ruin, pungent with the thousands of unburied corpses and noisy with the shouts of looters.

The surrender of the King of Delhi to Hodson.

143

Chapter 9

Havelock's Column

The news of Delhi's recapture was received with joy in Calcutta where Canning's popularity had plunged to the depths. The residents, resentful of his moderation and caution, sent a petition to the Queen demanding his removal. Members of Masonic Lodges, trade associations, French and other foreign communities demanded to be allowed to enlist in a volunteer corps, but Canning rejected them all, feeling that they would not be efficient soldiers. Nicknamed '"Clemency" Canning' for his moderation, he was proved right in this because the vindictiveness with which the Mutiny was now being suppressed only served to encourage resistance to the last man and was to cost more British lives than necessary.

But the British were smarting under their humiliations and were demanding action; their minds – even those of priests – were full of loathing for the Indians. The first stories of the Mutiny and the defeat of British soldiers had been read with disbelief. Then, when the newspapers filled their columns with stories of women boiled alive in butter and children barbecued, of slices cut from babies and forced into their mothers' mouths, letters to *The Times* demanded that not one stone in Delhi should be left standing on another. The Americans – no lovers of the British in those days, but faced with an Indian problem of their own – gave their stern opinion of the rebels and the Pope demanded a world fund for the sufferers. Even in France, which, a century before flung out of India by Clive, might well have enjoyed the sight of the new conquerors humbled, Napoleon III agreed that Britain's reinforcements should be allowed to cross the country to Marseilles in order to reach India more quickly.

The Mutiny was being carried on with bestial ferocity on both sides. The sepoys did not hesitate to murder and the British, as they caught up with them, did not hesitate to hang without trial. Both sides were afraid, the Indians of reprisals, the British – though they never admitted it – of a people far more numerous than they were. Because of the fear, violence had bred on violence in a climate of hysteria until the whole of Northern India had become a ruin of shattered towns and burned villages, and even loyal retainers had gone in danger of their lives. Lieutenant Mackenzie's bearer was almost killed because of his natty turban and martial whiskers and he had to be told to take the curl out of his moustaches and drop his jaunty gait and 'generally look as dirty as possible'.

In the hatred that sprang from the murder of women and children, twenty-one princes of the imperial family were hanged at

Opposite
Reinforcements were hurried up country to Lucknow.

145

Delhi after a travesty of a trial. The new troops who came out from England assumed that everyone with a black face was a murderer and had to be restrained from fixing bayonets and killing every male Indian they saw. Even a man as intelligent as the future Field-Marshal Lord Wolseley was able to say of the things he saw in Delhi, 'Had any Christian bishop visited that scene of butchery . . . he would have buckled on his sword.'

Delhi, the symbol of the overthrow of British rule, had been regained and Wilson now moved his headquarters to the palace. Seeing the place from the inside, amazed at its strength, he wrote to his wife, 'Most certainly to the Lord of Hosts can be ascribed the victory.' Despite the Almighty's help, however, it had been a costly affair. On the British side alone 3,835 men had been killed, wounded or missing from May to September – 2,140 of them Europeans – while how many civilians or rebels, who had fought with no less devotion and daring, laid down their lives or were killed without trial could never be known. Among the survivors the attitude was not the attitude of England or Calcutta. It was one of simple relief that it was all over and they were alive. Lieutenant Edward Thackeray, a cousin of the novelist, wrote, 'I am sick of bloodshed and seeing men killed,' while Edward Vibart, who had seen the horrors from the very first day of the outbreak at Delhi when he had fled over the ramparts, wrote, 'Please God I may never see such a bloody and awful sight again.'

Those who were ordered away from the city to chase the fleeing mutineers and join other campaigns considered themselves lucky, because in Delhi they were still dragging out swollen corpses worried by dogs or torn by vultures too gorged to move, and the atmosphere was poisonous with decay and the stench of death. The air seemed to Captain George Bourchier to be 'dense and uncomfortable to breathe', and the sandbags and wreckage that lay everywhere and the abandoned guns, loaded to the muzzles, showed how willing the mutineers had been to fight.

Cholera was still claiming victims, and those still on their feet, after months of 'bad food, bad water, bad everything', were exhausted, dilapidated and ill and Baird Smith found himself 'as weak as a child'.

The looting had been tremendous with men stumbling over shattered mirrors and broken furniture, carrying jewels, carpets and Kashmir shawls. Often it led to blows and even bloodshed between white and native troops as they completed the devastation wrought by the rebels and the city's rabble and broke up every article of furniture they could find in the wealthy Indian houses and

The looting at Delhi
was tremendous.

threw it into the streets so that they became blocked as though by
vast barricades. The place was like a city of the dead, and as it
suddenly dawned on them that the streets were deserted they
began asking themselves what had become of the thousands of
inhabitants. They were discovered days later, hiding in cellars,
half-starved and terrified of both British and rebels. There was no
means of feeding them and because of a fear of plague they were
turned out of the city with the information that food was being
provided for them. 'We had our doubts on the subject,' Griffiths
said, 'and knowing how callous . . . the authorities had become, I
fear that many perished from want and exposure.'

The jackals gnawed at the bodies of sepoys and civilians rotting
in the sun, where they were allowed to lie until the stench became
unbearable. The city was an empty shell. Mrs Muter, one of the
first Englishwomen into it, noticed that the palace was a sad picture
of dilapidation and filth. She was shown the gallows where rich and
poor were hanged, and also saw a well into which young Indian
girls of high birth had flung themselves as the troops advanced.

Nicholson had died on the 23rd and had been buried on the 24th,
without bands or volleys of musketry. The Englishmen who stood
watching were sun-dried or white with fever and sickness. Among
them were the Pathans, Afghans and Multanis who had worshipped
him, and as the clods of earth fell on the coffin the Multanis flung
themselves on the ground like children in their anguish and cried
without restraint. With Nicholson gone, however, they owed no 147

allegiance to anyone and after the funeral they returned to their homes, laden with as much loot as they could carry.

Though Delhi was no longer there as a symbol round which the mutineers could rally, there was still a lot to do.

As August had worn on, the behaviour of men like Neill, who had acted with brutality, had driven the isolated units of mutineers together to make a rebellion which stretched the whole length of the Grand Trunk Road from Calcutta to the Punjab – one thousand miles of territory, five hundred miles wide. Feudal barons had begun to seize the reins again and collect their own revenue, supported by a formidable army of people demanding their freedom – not only soldiers but repressed priests, servants, shopkeepers and peasants. Despite John Lawrence's firm grip in the Punjab, he was short of soldiers now and few Sikhs from the Punjab had yet joined the colours because the whole of Northern India had been watching Delhi. The situation had all along remained touch and go with the wily princes in contact with both sides until Delhi fell, and by this time the plight of the garrison of the Residency in Lucknow was growing desperate. Surrounded by a vast city full of rebellious elements which included large numbers of skilled soldiers and artillerymen, they still held out. But, short now of food, candles, soap and the simplest necessities of life, they were beginning to suffer from 'garrison disease' – the ailment of shortage – with boils, scurvy, weakness, and wounds that would not heal. Rations were cut again and the numbers of the defenders dwindled.

Shot and shell had rained down constantly on the defences, and on 11 August, part of the Residency had collapsed and half a dozen men were buried. The rebels, crawling through the long grass that was growing swiftly in the merciless rain, had kept up a constant sniping, and from time to time small storming parties of the defenders had had to attack enemy strongpoints which crept too close. It was not long before they had become aware of a new danger – mining – as strange scraping noises were detected by women beneath the floors of the cellars where they sheltered. The miners were driven back from their points of entrance by storming parties but by the middle of August they were back again.

On 10 August, a tremendous attack by 1,600 howling sepoys with scaling ladders was launched and a mine tore away 60 feet of the defences. The assault was fought off by the desperate defenders, the hard-pressed gunners sprinting from gun to gun. Losses increased

At Lucknow, the
defenders had to combat
a new form of attack –
mining. The first sounds
were heard by women
in the cellars.

daily and by 1 September, after two months of siege, over three
hundred Europeans had died of wounds or sickness. Everyone kept
up their efforts to remain cheerful, however; the women played their
traditional Victorian role looking after the nursing, reading the
Bible to the wounded and the sick, caring for the children, providing entertainment in the evening whenever possible with songs,
pretending that all would soon be well.

But by now their children were growing large-eyed, sickly and
weak, wizened with hunger and fear, and as indifferent to the death
they saw around them as their parents. There was no milk for the
babies and those women like Julia Inglis who had a goat had to
refuse the milk to desperate mothers because they knew that there
was only enough for their own children, and despite all the efforts
made on their behalf the innocent victims of the tragedy continued
to die of malnutrition and dysentery.

Women who had not done a thing for themselves in years now
found themselves occupied constantly with the chores of washing,
cooking, cleaning and looking after the sick, their only comfort in
the dark nights by the light of a candle the talk of England. One
after the other they died, of cholera, smallpox and dysentery, whole
families being wiped out, first the husband, shot down in the defences, then the exhausted wife, and finally the orphaned little ones.
Whenever the bombardments began, the women repaired to the
cellars where, in clouds of dust and in darkness, they could only   149

clutch the screaming children and wait in terror for the end. Their strength came from their sentimental faith, and 'We are in the hands of God' was a phrase that was repeated in letters and journals time after time.

By now, the Indian soldiers of the garrison were becoming a problem. They were suspected of being in contact with the rebels and some of them had actually deserted, and men of uncertain loyalty were posted to those places where they could not easily escape. The Indians knew they were not trusted and began now to suspect that the messenger who had risked his life again and again to take messages out was merely a figment of British imagination designed to keep their spirits up with the information that Havelock was at hand.

Havelock's problems were immense, however. On 17 August he had been informed – not officially but through a newspaper – that he had been superseded in command by Major-General Sir James Outram. Although to unknowing people it seemed hard on him, in fact he didn't regard it as odd. Outram, an old friend, was a short, florid, man with dark grizzled hair, christened because of his courage, kindliness and manliness 'the Bayard of India'. Always as courteous to the wife of a private soldier as he was to the wife of a general, he was a genial man regarded with great affection by children and by his younger officers, but he was still a man of decision, courage and intelligence. He had been Havelock's commander in Persia and, as the size of the forces available for the relief of Lucknow grew, he, a more senior officer, had come to take over. Appointed Chief Commissioner for Oudh, the civil as well as the military commander, he was to control all troops in the central area of the Ganges. With him as Chief of Staff was Colonel Robert Napier, the future Lord Napier of Magdala, a soldier of rare ability.

Leaving Calcutta on 6 August, he made his way north, organising the troops along the way as he went. Reaching Allahabad on 2 September he despatched reinforcements ahead of him to Havelock whose effective strength was now reduced by disease to 700, while the rebels, encouraged by his failures, had been growing in numbers all the time. Oppressed by the feeling that if Lucknow fell more rebels would be released to attack him, the little general wrote to Calcutta saying that he was considering retreating to Allahabad, though with reinforcements to bring his force up to between two and three thousand, he felt he could hold his position.

In Calcutta by now also was Sir Colin Campbell, who had taken over as Commander-in-Chief, India, from Sir Patrick Grant, who had made the first countrywide organisational moves. Thinking in

Sir James Outram.

150

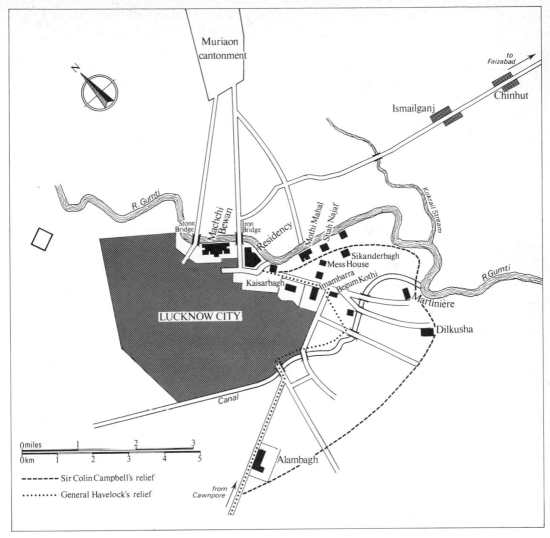

Map of Lucknow showing Muriaon cantonment, R. Gumti, Stone Bridge, Machchi Bewan, Iron Bridge, Residency, Mothi Mahal, Shah Najaf, Kokrail Stream, Ismailganj, Chinhut, to Faizabad, Sikanderbagh, Mess House, Kaisarbagh, Imambarra, Begum Kothi, Martinière, Dilkusha, LUCKNOW CITY, Canal, Alambagh, from Cawnpore.

0 miles 1   2   3
0 km   1   2   3   4   5

- - - - - - Sir Colin Campbell's relief

· · · · · · · General Havelock's relief

terms of reconstruction rather than quelling the mutiny, Grant had
remained all the time at Canning's side but Campbell had been
sent by Lord Palmerston – always the most jingoistic of Englishmen
and a firm believer in gunboat diplomacy – to settle the matter
once and for all. He had been a fighting soldier from his earliest
days in the army. A veteran of the Napoleonic Wars, he was the son
of a Glasgow carpenter who had been educated by a wealthy uncle
and had fought in the Second Sikh War and later in the Crimea
where he was one of the few soldiers to emerge with an untarnished
reputation. He had so distinguished himself there, in fact, he had
been accorded the highest of British honours by having public
houses named after him. Nevertheless, he was far from young and

though his soldiers thought him 'a regular go-ahead, fire-eating old cock', he had also been called by Nicholson 'that old ass' and he was to make more than one mistake. However, he had the confidence of his men and the wild cheering of the 93rd Highlanders, whom he had led at Balaclava, as they saw him, indicated his popularity.

The outlook was by no means encouraging, though. Cawnpore was held only with difficulty and Lucknow and other outstations were still besieged, while too many of the reinforcements Campbell had brought had to be frittered away in small numbers to hold important posts en route to the north. There was hardly any transport in Calcutta, few horses for the cavalry or artillery, little ammunition and a shortage of flour. However, Allahabad remained in British hands and he had acted at once, sending on the reinforcements Havelock demanded which were passed on by Outram as he travelled north. Nevertheless Outram was not able to bring with him as many men as he had hoped owing to the situation remaining around Dinapur. He left Allahabad on 5 September, intending to march fast to Havelock's assistance but the heat knocked out so many of his men he soon had to reduce his speed.

On arrival, he at once informed Havelock that, despite his superior rank, he did not intend to deprive him of the command and the glory of relieving Lucknow, for which he had strived so long, but in fact, he did not always leave everything to him and interfered when he felt it necessary. Yet, in his kindness, he also allowed the impulsive Havelock to reject good advice and make mistakes.

Havelock's force now numbered nearly 3,200 men, of whom nearly 2,400 were European. He was still sadly lacking in cavalry, but there were three batteries of artillery, one British and two Indian which enabled him to reorganise the force into two brigades.

The bridge of boats was reconstructed and on 18 September, as the battle for Delhi was reaching its climax, three guns were passed across the Ganges and were immediately engaged with the mutineers' artillery on the other side which they silenced after a three-hour duel. The following day the rest of the force crossed the river. During his wait, Havelock had been constructing special carriages to transport boats for the crossing of the Rivers Sai and Gumti which had held him up in his previous advances and, as the army prepared in heavy rain on the night of the 19th for an advance, the last of the guns crossed the river. The mutineers were still at Mangalwar across the main road and, as Havelock opened fire with the heavy guns, Outram led a body of cavalry through blinding rain against the mutineers' flank, capturing two guns.

Bashiratganj, the scene of Havelock's three earlier battles, had

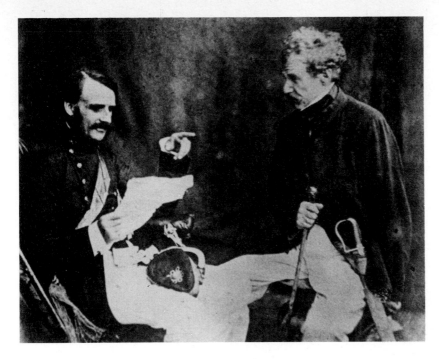

Sir Colin Campbell
(later Lord Clyde) with
Major-General Sir
William Mansfield.

been deserted by the fleeing rebels, and the next day, in a deluge
of rain, he marched beyond it to the banks of the Sai. The boats he
had brought were not necessary as the rebels had left the bridge
undestroyed and Havelock crossed at once and camped within
sixteen miles of Lucknow. There he fired a salvo of artillery to warn
the defenders but, as the rebels were shelling the defences at the
time, it was not heard.

On the following day the force moved off again through steaming
heat and as the guns which had been thudding from the direction
of Lucknow could no longer be heard it was assumed that the enemy
was preparing to fight off the relief force. As they reached the Alambagh, a pleasure garden and palace of the kings of Oudh, they came
upon the enemy's line. It stretched for two miles, its left on the
Alambagh, its right and centre behind a chain of small hills. There
were 10,000 infantry and 1,500 cavalry but, despite the strength of
the position and the fact that it was impossible to get at the enemy's
right flank because of a marsh, the British advanced. The enemy's
cavalry were the first to break and soon the whole native army was
in retreat, pursued by Outram with the few British horsemen.

They were cheered by the news which arrived that Delhi had
fallen but the divided command was causing trouble. Neill, ruthless
but shrewd, thought that having two generals in command of a
handful of men was a 'farce', especially with one of them doing   153

nothing. Although Outram had promised not to interfere, when he gave advice it became a command, but he and Havelock disagreed about whether to take the tents with them and whether to use artillery in the final advance. In one, Outram overruled Have-

Flayed by fire,
Havelock's force
stormed through the
narrow streets of
Lucknow.

lock and in the other gave in, so that the troops were always uncertain whom to obey.

They had to push through a city of twelve square miles and the
route to be taken to the Residency was hotly debated throughout

24 September. One route was by a road which had been heavily entrenched and was lined with loopholed houses. A less direct but safer route on the other side of the river was rejected because, after the rain, it was felt it would be impossible to get the artillery across the soaked ground. A third plan suggested by Outram, who knew the area well because he had once been Resident and Chief Commissioner in Lucknow, also had the disadvantage that the rebels were strongly established in houses overlooking the route. Outram's route was finally decided on, and the baggage, sick and wounded were left in the Alambagh under the protection of some three hundred soldiers, while the heavy guns, on Havelock's insistence, were taken.

On the morning of 25 September, the force moved off, to come at once under heavy fire from high grass and two-storeyed houses and garden walls. The strongpoint was carried but almost immediately another was faced at a point where the British artillery could not be brought up. Despite one setback after another, the force pressed on, flayed by fire, men losing their way in the narrow streets and finding themselves face to face with immense numbers of mutineers. They still had not reached the perimeter of the Residency defences as night began to fall and the position began to look desperate. With the Residency only three-quarters of a mile away they paused to draw breath, wounded and stragglers dotting the route behind them and much of the artillery by which Havelock had set such store stuck in the mud. Outram demanded a halt, feeling that a few hours' pause would allow the rearguard to close up and enable them to consolidate their present position and advance to the Residency through the intervening palaces. It was not a method of dash or brilliancy, he thought, but at least it would have kept losses to a minimum. Havelock, impulsive as ever and believing Outram was proposing an all-night halt at a time when he felt the Residency's defences were in danger of giving way, insisted on an immediate advance. Though they would be hard hit, he said, they would do the thing quickly and get it over and, angrily, Outram retorted 'Let us go then, in God's name!'

It was an unfortunate decision because every foot of the way ahead bristled with muskets and field guns. The loopholed houses were full of rebels and deep trenches had been cut across the streets and, jammed together as they were, the relieving column was a perfect target. With Havelock and Outram, who was by now wounded in the arm, at their head, they pushed on, flayed by the fusillade of fire. Although the guns of the Residency were turned on the rebel positions, the advance was akin to the charge of the Light

Brigade at Balaclava, and the few cavalry with them were unable to
help because they were all carrying wounded. Of the 2,000 men
who took part in the final advance, 535 became casualties, some of
the wounded dragged away by rebels as the column passed, to be
murdered down the dark alleys or burned to death in their litters
as they lay helpless. Among the dead was Neill, falling from his
horse shot through the head. Oddly enough, despite his reputation,
he had been one of the few officers to think of providing sweetmeats
for the children of Lucknow and small comforts for the women.

A last desperate rush brought them to the Residency where Sikh
defenders trying to open a breach for them to enter by were
bayoneted by mistake as they rose to greet them, then they were
inside and the defenders went mad with joy. The senior officers
had more to think about. Though they dined on hoarded mock
turtle soup, beef cutlets and champagne, Havelock was depressed
by his losses and wept unashamedly as the stragglers came in. And,
because of Outram's unwillingness to overrule him on the question
of the final advance, the whole point of their arrival had been lost.

It had been intended all along to evacuate the Residency but,
such were their losses, that was now clearly impossible and all that
had happened was that the relieving force in many ways had merely
increased the problems of the garrison. Despite the courage, the
Residency still had to be relieved.

Chapter 10

The Relief of Lucknow

Treasure and valuables were still being dug up at Delhi and courts martial were sentencing soldiers and civilians alike to death. But even as they drew breath after the battle and counted the cost in dead and wounded, the needs of hard-pressed garrisons in other parts of the country were not forgotten and a column was organised to relieve Agra, 160 miles away along the Jumna. The column, 2,650 strong, 750 British among them, left under Brigadier Greathed on 24 September.

The headquarters of the civil government in the North-West Provinces, Agra was another Moghul fortress and the garrison consisted of the 3rd Bengal Fusiliers, a recently raised, inexperienced British regiment. As the outlying districts had fallen to the mutineers and since many of the Fusiliers were away on sick leave, the two native infantry battalions who had made up the garrison with a battery of European artillery were disarmed, and the British inhabitants moved into the fort.

The Lieutenant-Governor, John Colvin, was an able, intelligent civil servant of long standing who had done all he could to exploit the differences between Muslims and Hindus. But his health had broken under the strain, and there was constant discord between civil and military and a foolish attempt to attack a force of mutineers approaching the area ended in a defeat as bad as Chinhut. As the mob rose the British were confined entirely to the fort, only allowing loyal Indians and Eurasians to join them when they found they could not look after their daily needs without servants.

Agra was not besieged but there were constant alarms, many of them false. There were no sanitary arrangements and the fort was full of filth, and the garrison, believing it to contain the hidden hoards of the Moghuls, spent their time in vain treasure hunts. Nevertheless, they were quite safe there from anything but a major attack, but as Greathed approached the appeals for help grew strident and as he entered the city without opposition on 11 October he decided that the vast force which was said to be threatening the fort was purely a figment of the imagination. His men were worn, sun-dried skeletons already exhausted by their exertions at Delhi, but to their disgust they found that the soldiers in Agra were smartly dressed in scarlet and pipe clay and that their women were wearing fashionable clothes. Told by the city's intelligence officers that the rebel force which had been threatening the city had moved away as he had approached, Greathed was deceived by the apparent security of the garrison and allowed himself to be caught unawares as he made camp. His men rallied, however, and the

Opposite
Thomas Henry
Kavanagh.

159

mutineers were routed with the loss of all their baggage and guns.

His orders now were to push on to Cawnpore where the situation was known to be serious. A long-delayed message, delivered by a fakir in his food bowl, indicated that Havelock was heading for Lucknow and begged any British commander who read the message to push on as fast as possible to his assistance. There was great need for help. Despite the relief, Lucknow was not much better off.

Though Havelock's men had behaved with incredible heroism, it was felt that the whole business of the advance to the Residency had been a 'muddle, however gloriously conducted, from beginning to end'. According to Inglis's aide, Outram 'did not seem pleased with the conduct of operations', but Outram had been as guilty as anyone of misjudgement.

A host of legends were woven around the defence and relief of the city. Many of them sprang from the imagination of reporters and the desire of the Victorians for something to redeem the squalid horror of the Mutiny. The flag that was supposed never to have been lowered – it flew for generations afterwards as a symbol, never leaving the top of the staff even at sunset – in fact spent most of its time at the bottom because it was so regularly shot down. The story of the wife of a Highland soldier who dreamed of hearing the pipes of the relieving Scots, which produced poems, ballads and paintings, was similarly pure imagination.

The bad organisation gave rise to such muddles as Inglis's belief that his garrison was on the verge of starvation when, in fact, below the Residency building there was a vast swimming bath packed with supplies. They had been placed there by Lawrence but he had not informed the commissariat officers and had died before he could tell them. They were found by one of the relieving force.

At least, however, the discovery meant that the contemplated retreat of Outram's force to the Alambagh was no longer necessary, and, in addition, the weather was cooler and the garrison was bigger than it had been and was more able to stave off attacks. But the hospitals were now more full than ever, many of the patients men wounded during Havelock's final advance through the narrow streets of the city. Their arrival had brought other tragedies also, as news was given of husbands and brothers who had died. One of the more poignant cases was that of Mrs Katherine Bartrum, whose child was weak and thin and was eventually to die, and whose husband, a handsome military surgeon whom she adored, had been shot through the head just outside the Residency gates.

Outram resumed command on the day after the relief and Inglis was given command of the Residency proper, while Havelock took over the captured palaces and buildings to the east with which the perimeter had been extended. It was not a good defensive position, because the additional perimeter had left a gap without proper defences and was exposed to constant musketry and gunfire, while the arrival of the new force had not, as Outram had hoped, discouraged the rebels in the slightest.

A force left behind in the Alambagh to guard the route to safety was still cut off and, though messengers were always able to get through, it was quite clear that any attempt to break out was out of the question. And with the wounded that Havelock's impulsiveness and Outram's casualness about command had caused, there were now a thousand sick, women and children to care for. 'Two additional brigades with powerful field artillery will be required to withdraw,' Outram reported.

At last, however, it seemed possible that such a force might be raised. An alarmed England was pouring troops into India for a final rescue and to put down the rebellion before it spread across the whole sub-continent. The fury and hatred of the Victorians had been immense and William Howard Russell, convinced all the way to India about the stories of horror, was determined to find out how much truth there was in them. He found it surprisingly difficult. 'I wanted proof,' he wrote, 'but none was forthcoming. All the stories we heard were from Calcutta, and the people of Calcutta were far from the districts where, no doubt, most treacherous and wholesale murder had been perpetrated.' He found it hard to believe the stories of mutilation and of white women being blown from guns and children used as target practice, but he *did* believe them. At Calcutta, however, he saw wounded men, with stumps of legs and arms which he thought, after his experience in the Crimea, were the result of round shot. It turned out, though, that they had been lopped off in battle by the razor-sharp swords of the mutineers.

The troops who were now arriving had no knowledge of the country, its languages or its problems, and, in their hatred and thirst for vengeance, they killed Indians on the slightest provocation, even though they could not possibly have been involved in any of the atrocities; while officers, lacking experience in the ways of the Indian army, even made the mistake of hanging their own servants because they did not know who they were and, seeing them loitering near their quarters to await their master's call, thought they were looking for a chance to murder them. Hundreds of miles from the uprisings there were unnecessary killings of innocent natives. 'I seed two Moors talking in a cart,' a soldier said. 'Presently I heard one of them say "Cawnpore". I knowed what that meant; so I fetched Tom Walker, and he heard 'em say "Cawnpore" and he knowed what that meant. So we polished 'em both off.'

The need, however, was less for reprisals than for haste. In Lucknow, despite the discovery in the swimming bath, rations were still desperately short and, as they were cut again to provide for all the extra men Outram had brought, people began to dream of food, and even sparrows were being caught to help out the rations where once a peacock had been allowed to go free because of its beauty.

Apart from the lucky few, most of the defenders had forgotten what comfort was. Assailed by sharpshooter fire every time they left shelter, the buildings ravaged by shot and shell, they had lost all sense of time and the value of money, and the smallest things – an unexpected egg, a swig of liquor or a smoke – brought enormous pleasure. They were all filthy and tired and Outram was full of concern for his command, while Havelock, his greatest moment past, was sick and showing signs of weakening. The hospital was appalling by now as bandages were used and re-used and women gave up their undergarments to take their place. There was a desperate shortage of drugs and operations were performed in the most unhygienic conditions in full view of the other patients. In the absence of knowledge, amputation was the answer for everything but, because of gangrene, pyoemia and simple lack of strength after the long siege, they were almost always fatal, and with infection rampant, most of the defenders preferred to keep their minor sicknesses and injuries to themselves.

Always in their minds was the thought of final relief. Hundreds had died and they were still dying, and, though the defending force had grown with Outram's reinforcements to 2,700, it was believed that the rebels outside still numbered not less than 60,000 – 32,000 of them retainers of feudal princes. Both the siege and the defence had now for the most part become one of mining, and as soldiers who had fought bravely in all the numerous battles of the defence and the attempt at relief found they could not face the darkness underground, new heroes were thrown up who could. Among them was Thomas Henry Kavanagh, a low-paid civilian clerk who had spent most of his life in debt but now, having fought bravely through the siege, conducted counter-mining operations so successfully Outram dubbed him 'the assistant field engineer'. He spent hours below ground with Cornish miners serving in the 32nd, blowing in the rebels' mines as they approached the defences, even fighting them with pistols in the candle-lit darkness.

On 6 November, spirits rose as Hope Grant was reported across the Sai and awaiting Sir Colin Campbell from Cawnpore. He was already in touch with the force at the Alambagh and a semaphore signal station was set up. The instructions on how to work it were found in an encyclopaedia in Martin Gubbins' library, and suggestions were sent by Outram for the attack of the relieving force.

By now they were well into November and the Residency had been under siege for over four months and everyone was terrified that the new attempt at relief, through lack of knowledge of the best route, would end as disastrously as the first. It was at this point that Kavanagh, despite the fact that he was tall and had golden hair, offered to make his way through to the relieving force disguised as a native and guide it through the city to the Residency. Outram was at first doubtful of his ability to disguise himself but, his skin stained with lampblack mixed with oil and wearing clothes collected from various Indian members of the defence, Kavanagh left with a native guide on 9 November and reached Campbell's force the next morning. For this he was eventually promoted to judge with an increase in salary and, though a civilian, was given the Victoria Cross.

How the miners waited for the Indians to break through.

163

Benefiting from the reorganisations made by Sir Patrick Grant,
Campbell had been thinking all along in terms of a final suppression
of the Mutiny. He needed cavalry and rations, however, and was
well aware that, although British forces had moved north, in their
haste they had been able to do nothing to pacify the country
through which they had passed. Believing that Outram would bring
out the defenders of Lucknow, he had intended to deal with all
these problems before moving north himself but, with Outram also
now shut up in Lucknow and in the incorrect belief that the garrison
was starving, he decided to march off at once. Of the reliable commanders, there was only Hope Grant available and on 27 October,
with his Chief of Staff, Mansfield, he set off north, arriving on 3
November at Cawnpore to join his troops.

His men were in the right frame of mind. They had been shown
Wheeler's entrenchment and the barracks where there were still
the remains of women's and children's clothing, broken toys, torn
164 pictures, books and pieces of music. Corporal William Forbes-

Mitchell, of the 93rd Highlanders, even found a New Testament in Gaelic from which leaves had been torn out – he believed for use as gun-waddings. They were also shown the Sati Chowra Ghat where the massacre at the boats had taken place and where many skeletons were still lying unburied among the bushes; and the Bibigahr where they were told of the Nana Sahib's black treachery in trying to persuade Mohammedan bakers to poison the British before the uprising with arsenic in their bread.

The room had not been cleaned out and the floors were still covered with congealed blood, and littered with the torn, trampled dresses of women and children, shoes, slippers and locks of long hair, many with parts of the scalp still attached. Everything had been left as it was to arouse in them a feeling of vengeance, and they were shown an iron hook six feet from the floor and covered with dried blood, where marks and small handprints on the wall seemed to indicate that a child had been affixed by its neck. The Indians were still being made to lick the floor before being hanged though already Dr Munro, the surgeon of his regiment, was beginning to wonder if they were the ones who were guilty of the massacre. Forbes-Mitchell, a humane man, took the view that they were not and refused to allow his section to indulge in the practice of smearing captives with hog fat.

Campbell had no time to waste with vengeance either and promptly put a stop to the atrocities Neill had instituted. Placing in command Major-General Charles Ash Windham, a man with no knowledge of India but with a reputation from the Crimea as a fighting general, he left again on 9 November with 3,400 men. They had been arriving all the time, eager to get at the rebels and eager for vengeance, yet even here, even in Cawnpore, officers passing through could complain coldly of the incivility of the servants in the rest houses, or that there was no tablecloth or that they could not get a napkin at dinner.

Among Campbell's forces were a naval brigade led by Captain William Peel, son of a former Prime Minister, who commanded sailors and marines armed with heavy guns and rocket launchers; the blackened and service-worn field guns that had hammered at the walls of Delhi; a regiment of sun-baked lancers on their lean, hardy mounts; wild Sikh horsemen in loose, fawn-coloured garbs with long boots and coloured turbans; the usual weary, over-worked, footslogging British infantry; Punjabis, tall and fierce and eager for loot; and the Highlanders – seventy per cent of them Gaelic-speaking and with their own ministers and elders – who regarded Campbell as much their own as he regarded them as *his*   165

Captain Peel bringing
up the naval guns.

own. Convinced that the little column was doomed to extermina-
tion, the camp-followers, men who had taken up the handicrafts
of their fathers and grandfathers to serve the army, deserted them
at once, only the low-caste water-carriers and dhooly-bearers
remaining.

Hardly opposed, however, they arrived at the Alambagh on
12 November. It had been intended to enter the Residency at once
by the direct route but when Kavanagh arrived the plan was
changed and Campbell chose a route which avoided the narrow
streets where Havelock had suffered so much. By now, with reinforcements and the garrison of the Alambagh, he had 5,000 men
and 49 guns at his disposal. These were divided into five brigades
under the general direction of Hope Grant. The route suggested,
although it avoided narrow streets, involved the taking of strongpoints established in palaces or large houses.

Marching out of the Alambagh across the fields on 14 November,
they met their first opposition at the wall of the Dilkusha Park, a
picturesque area filled with browsing herds of deer and enclosing a
chateau-type palace. A masked battery of six guns opened fire but
Peel's 24-pounders came into action and the rebels fell back to the
Martinière College, a school for boys whose scholars were occupied
in the defence of the Residency. At the Martinière, two guns were

turned on the advancing British cavalry but again the British guns
silenced them and the rebels retreated across the canal with the
cavalry on their heels.

The Naval contingent
in action at the Dilkusha.

Garrisoning the school and occupying villages to protect his left,
Campbell prepared his next move and rebel attacks were driven
back into the city by artillery fire. The following day, with the air
chilly and damp, the heavy baggage and stores were brought up
from the Dilkusha and, in the evening, as shells from Peel's guns
were dropped along another route to deceive the mutineers,
Campbell planned to approach the Residency across the canal and
along the river bank round the heart of the native city. By semaphore he informed Outram of his plans and the defenders of Lucknow arranged to make a sortie in strength to meet him.

On the 16th the canal was crossed and the troops moved along
the bank of the river through thick woods to the Sikanderbagh,
another fortified palace. As Campbell wrote, it was a 'high-walled
enclosure of strong masonry . . . carefully loopholed . . .' and it was
protected by a fortified village, but advancing under fire, the artillery brought its guns to bear while the infantry forced the rebels out
of the village. As the artillery began to pound the Sikanderbagh
itself, Campbell made his men lie down behind a low mud wall.
'Lie down, Ninety-Third, lie down,' he shouted at his Scotsmen. 167

'Every man of you is worth his weight in gold to England today.'

A breach was made and Campbell turned to Ewart, commanding the 93rd. 'Bring on the tartan,' he said. 'Let my own lads at them!' The breach was stormed and then the whole regiment, like one man, swarmed over the wall with a tremendous yell of pent-up rage and ferocity. As Corporal Forbes-Mitchell said, it had become 'a horrible and brutalising war' of 'downright butchery' and there was no mercy and no quarter on either side. Aware that a namesake of his had captured an enemy eagle at Waterloo and remembering the murder of his cousin and his family at Cawnpore, Colonel Ewart cut down eight of the enemy in his fury and snatched up a rebel colour. When he brought the banner to Campbell, however, still excited with the hysteria of battle, wounded, his cap shot away and covered with blood and blackened with powder, all he got in the way of thanks was 'Damn your colours, sir! It is not your place to be taking colours; go back to your regiment this instant!'

The rebels in the Sikanderbagh, still wearing red jackets, pantaloon-like trousers and bell-shaped shakoes, were trapped, and the slaughter was appalling. In desperation, when they had discharged their muskets, they hurled them at the advancing Scots, bayonets-first like javelins, and then flung themselves under the Highlanders' weapons to slash at their legs with tulwars, struggling to kill their attackers even as they fell among the trampled flowers. In the chaos of yells, shots and screams and the wailing of bagpipes, the Indians were pushed steadily back by black-faced, panting men roaring 'Cawnpore, you bloody murderers! Cawnpore!' and grimly offering what they called a 'Cawnpore dinner' – a bayonet in the stomach. Breaking off the fight and trying to flee, the sepoys shattered their legs and spines as they leapt off high roofs to the ground. As the fighting died down, the few survivors tried in vain to hide under the heaving heaps of wounded and dying, and amid the litter of abandoned weapons and clothing and crushed blossom, it was found by a strange coincidence that 1,857 mutineers lay dead, some of them with their clothes on fire as they sprawled across their own cooking fires. Among them were men wearing the Punjab medal and over fifty men of the 71st Native infantry in possession of leave passes; they had been on furlough when their regiment had mutinied and had rejoined the colours to fight the British.

There was little feeling of compassion and no sense of horror. As they stood among the litter of smashed equipment in an atmosphere that was thick with smoke and the stink of burning bodies, the British felt only that it was 'a glorious sight to see the mass of bodies,

dead and wounded.' 'Didn't we get revenge!' one officer exulted.
'The first good revenge I have seen.'

The taste of the powder, as they had bitten the cartridges, had made the soldiers almost mad with thirst and, with the sun high overhead and suffering intensely in their feather bonnets and heavy kilts, the Highlanders began to gather under a fig tree in the centre of the inner court where several jars of cool water stood. Then Captain Dawson noticed that there were many British bodies round the tree and that they had all been shot through the top of the head, and he called to a private who went by the name of 'Quaker' Wallace to watch the top branches. Still quoting the psalms he had been chanting all through the fight, Wallace spotted a movement and fired and the body that fell to the ground, clad in red coat and rose-coloured silk trousers, was that of a woman armed with a heavy old-patterned cavalry pistol and a pouch half-full of ammunition. Despite her murderous activities, Wallace was stricken with remorse at killing a woman.

Ahead of the British now lay only the Shah Najaf mosque, situated in a garden enclosed by a high loopholed wall a quarter of a mile ahead. Between it and the Sikanderbagh across the rippling waves of heat was a patch of thick jungle and mud huts which hid the wall. Battered by Peel's artillery for three hours, the strongpoint was held by men who included among their number a group of archers armed with tremendously strong bows. Forbes-Mitchell saw one Highlander fall with an arrow clean through his skull, while a second arrow struck the body of another man with such force it passed clean through and dropped clear to the ground a few yards behind him.

The Highlanders entered through an unnoticed breach half-hidden by undergrowth, but as they rushed in they found the place deserted apart from a few bodies floating in the river, and it dawned on them that bugle calls they had imagined signified attacks had, in fact, signalled the rebels' retreat. It was Forbes-Mitchell who discovered why they had left so precipitately.

Despite the fires that lit up the foliage of the trees, the night was cold and, exhausted and hungry and seeking an abandoned greatcoat to combat the chill, he entered the mosque with a saucer of oil in which a twisted wick burned uncovered. To his horror he found himself knee-deep in enough loose gunpowder to blow them all to Kingdom Come. There was about forty hundredweight of the 169

explosive, in addition to unopened barrels and dozens of shells, all loaded and with the fuses fixed. He backed out hardly daring to breathe. It seemed that the defenders of the Residency had set up a battery to pound the mosque and, afraid that the artillery on one side or the other would blow up their store of gunpowder, the rebels had slipped silently away. As he lay down, still shaking, Forbes-Mitchell could hear other men about him, their minds still full of the excitement and horrors of the day, muttering in their sleep. 'Charge! Give them the bayonet,' they were saying, and 'Remember Cawnpore'.

Campbell's men and the defenders of the Residency were now only a short distance apart but the area between them was well covered by musketry fire, and the rebels, in an attempt to cut Campbell's communications, had attacked the Martinière and the Dilkusha and were deployed against the Alambagh. Campbell decided to wait for daylight, and Outram's first indication that relief was imminent was the arrival of Kavanagh in the defences wearing a staff officer's tunic and a pith helmet.

The following morning, as the relief force prepared for the last effort, it seemed as if the rebels were about to attack them. But nothing happened and Campbell, protecting his left and rear against an attack from the Kaisarbagh Palace sent in an attack against another palace, the Mothi Mahal. His naval guns pounded the Mess House, a large stone building dominating the Shah Najaf, and about 3 pm it was carried with a rush. Fred Roberts – 'Plucky Wee Bobs' to the Highlanders – who was to become a field marshal and a Commander-in-Chief, India, himself, handed over a Union Jack to be hoisted above the post. But when it was twice shot down, Campbell ordered the nonsense to stop because it was attracting too much fire.

An open space nearly half a mile wide and covered by musketry fire was still between the defenders and the relieving force but, impulse once more giving way to commonsense, Outram, Havelock and Kavanagh and six other officers set off across it to meet Campbell. Almost immediately four of them were wounded and had to crawl to the Mothi Mahal for cover while Kavanagh again made the dash to Campbell and brought the two groups together. After a discussion in which Campbell informed Havelock of a knighthood which had been conferred upon him, they set off back, Outram wheezing with asthma, Havelock leaning weakly on the arm of an aide and unable to run. Campbell had given them two hours to leave the Residency.

The news was received by the survivors while they were still delirious with joy at the thought of relief and enjoying trivial things like the taste of an orange or the chance to see a newspaper. It deflated them at once. To the sentimental Victorians, the thought of leaving the bodies of husbands, children and wives still buried within the Residency was heartbreaking, but Campbell gave them no alternative. With all their sick, wounded, women and children, the task had seemed impossible to Outram and Havelock who felt that the rebels should be driven at least from the Kaisarbagh first and that Campbell should then hold the city. Campbell, however, had decided that a strong force outside the city was as good a way of holding the rebels as any. With five hundred casualties already, it did not make sense to garrison the Residency once more and submit to another siege, and he had learned that the mutineers of the Gwalior Contingent were already threatening his retreat at Cawnpore. With his ammunition running low, he preferred to remain at the Alambagh, from where he could attack the city when he felt strong enough, and pass back the garrison with its procession of sick, wounded and civilians along his chain of outposts, withdrawing the troops behind him as he went.

Where open spaces left the evacuation exposed to enemy fire, an attempt was made to conceal the route with tents and canvas hung up as screens. Behind them a ditch was dug along which the garrison could walk in safety. Despite their ordeal, the women refused to leave their treasures and, with silver and other valuables sewn into their clothes and wearing sometimes as many as three of every garment, they set off on 19 November, some of them insisting on taking their best china, their lace wedding dresses or even a dead husband's harmonium. A few managed to ride on ponies or even in carriages drawn by half-starved horses, but Inglis's wife stubbornly walked every step of the way, feeling indignantly that transport should be occupied only by the sick.

The retreat was not well managed, despite the reports of contemporary journalists, and there was a great deal of luck involved. Fortunately they were not harassed by the rebels but far too much attention was paid to private whims and far too much time was occupied with women who clung selfishly or sentimentally to their possessions. One woman wore so many clothes she had to be hoisted on and off her pony, and some of them, narrow-minded and snobbish even at this tense hour of deliverance, managed to behave badly, one of them haughtily refusing the plea of a dying private for water. Overhearing them criticising the inadequate transport, Campbell turned on them. He had long since lost patience with some of them. There was a story that when, on arrival, he had

been regaled by the élite of the garrison with a meal of hoarded
foodstuffs and champagne, he had enquired frostily why it hadn't
been handed over to the troops and had sat with his arms folded
throughout the whole dreadful repast like a ghost at the feast. But
the instincts of self-preservation that the long siege had brought
out remained hard to throw off, and one young officer, who had
procured a chicken with great difficulty to supplement his meagre
rations, had it stolen by a boy of five who, it appeared, 'wanted it
for his mother'.

At the Sikanderbagh, where the rebel dead still lay, a prey to
vultures and jackals, they were given the first decent food many of
them had seen for months, and wide-eyed children excitedly drew
their mothers' attention to the fact that there was real bread on the
tables. Two days later at midnight on 22 November, Inglis's weary

garrison began its own retreat. Inglis claimed the right to be the last to leave, though he and Outram left together. Even then they were not the last. Captain Waterman, of the 13th Native Infantry, one of the rearguard, had fallen asleep with exhaustion, and when he awoke he found everyone had gone. There was not a sound among the ruins, not a movement in the darkness, and the shock of the weird desolation so unhinged his mind that he had to be sent home under escort.

By this time the civilians had reached the Dilkusha. They arrived in the early hours of the 23rd, when Havelock, already weak and ill, was struck down by dysentery. He died in the arms of his son on the 24th, and was buried at the Alambagh, within sight of his triumph.

The revenge of the British. Mutineers were blown from guns.

173

Chapter 11

The Scent
of Victory

The news of the relief spread across the country-side to Calcutta and the north and soon reached the Middle East. Troops coming out as reinforcements heard of it at Alexandria as shipping agents' boats came alongside their transports. The news they brought was electric. 'Lucknow is relieved,' they shouted, and the ships' decks became scenes of wild enthusiasm.

But, though Lucknow's garrison had been plucked to safety, Campbell's problems had been by no means solved. He still had to shepherd his convoy of 2,000 sick, wounded and civilians through a countryside swarming with enemies ready at any moment to fall on it and slaughter every man, woman and child, and he had only 3,000 men to guard it. Having left 4,000 men with 25 guns and 10 mortars at the Alambagh as the nucleus of a force to be raised for the resumption of the offensive against Lucknow, he was trying to get to Cawnpore, but he had not heard from Windham for four days and was beginning to suspect that he was in trouble.

Reaching the bridge over the River Sai on the evening of 27 November, he learned that gunfire had been heard, and began to force the pace in fear that his crossing of the Ganges would be threatened. The distant firing grew louder at every moment and the weary soldiers pricked up their ears and stepped out grimly. A message was received at last, written as usual with Greek phrases interspersing the English. It was two days old and was from Windham to announce that the Cawnpore garrison had been in-volved in severe fighting against an enemy powerful in all arms, especially artillery. Unless help came soon, Windham went on, he would have to retire.

Windham's instructions had been clear and had covered every contingency. With his small force of five hundred Europeans and a few Sikhs, he was to occupy and improve Neill's old entrenchment near the bridge of boats and watch for the mutineers of the Gwalior Contingent. If reinforcements arrived, he was to pass them on to Campbell, while making as much fuss as he could to give the impres-sion that his own force was bigger than it was; but under no circum-stances was he to get involved in a fight except to protect the en-trenchment. While he had been strengthening his position, how-ever, Tantia Topi, lieutenant and military adviser to the Nana Sahib, had arrived at Kalpi, 46 miles away. 'A wary, capable astute man', he was a blunt-faced thirty-year-old and one of the few Indian military leaders thrown up by the Mutiny, and he was quick to act. Rightly believing that Campbell was fully occupied with

Opposite
Russell of *The Times*
watching the looting in
the Kaisarbagh.

175

Lucknow, he had moved at once to Cawnpore, cutting off Windham's communications to the north. Receiving permission to hang
on to reinforcements for his own use in the expectation of a rebel
attack, Windham sent forward on the 23rd a small force of native
infantry and two European-manned guns. His instructions were
that they were to reoccupy the bridge that Campbell would need
for his retreat, but he decided to meet Tantia Topi himself before
he reached the entrenchment.

Leaving a small force behind, he marched towards Kalpi with
1,200 infantry, 12 guns and 100 cavalry. Tantia Topi was too clever
for him, however. To meet him, he sent forward only 2,500
infantry, 500 cavalry and six heavy guns and, though Windham
put them to flight, he suddenly discovered that Tantia Topi's
main body was nearer than he thought and, receiving a message
that his position at Cawnpore was being attacked, he had no
alternative but to retreat to protect the city itself and the bridge
over the Ganges. With 20,000 rebels and 40 guns clamouring at his
heels, a panic among his young soldiers sent him and his force
tumbling into the entrenchment, leaving all his stores and baggage
and those of Campbell's force to be destroyed by the rebels.

Fortunately, Campbell arrived that evening, to be greeted by
demoralised troops and the flames of burning buildings, which
indicated how narrow Windham's escape had been. The following
day, a long dusty procession of limping soldiers, palanquins,
camels, bullock carts and litters containing the women, children,
sick and wounded from Lucknow arrived, the last crossing the
river on the last day of the month. Securing the bridge, Campbell
176   immediately began to evacuate them to Allahabad, and though

Tantia Topi was close by and in strength, by 3 December, the convoy was on its way.

The rebels did not leave Campbell alone, however, An attempt was made to destroy the bridge of boats by fire and an artillery bombardment of the British position was followed by a sudden attack. But Tantia Topi was careless, despite his skill, and his position was not a strong one, and Campbell saw that the town wall, which would give cover to his own men, would prevent movement of the enemy. Assisted by the guns of the vigorous Peel and his sailors, who somehow managed to advance with the skirmishers, he drove the rebels from their strongpoints, capturing every gun and ammunition cart they possessed, while General Mansfield, moving round the rebels' left, met and routed the forces of the Nana Sahib, who only just escaped with his life. He lost all his baggage and was driven through Bithur where his treasure was discovered hidden in a well.

Though no one knew it then, the turning point in the mutiny had at last been reached. The period of dread when the knowledge that defeat would bring only butchery and the British were waiting for the whole country to rise against them now changed subtly to one of victory. The country people, by producing the provisions they had been careful up to then to hide showed that they, too, knew which way the battles were likely to go in the future.

Despite the tragedies and despite the disasters, the mutiny had still never become a general uprising. Though many princes and their hangers-on and the bazaar thugs had joined, the peasants had continued to hang back and many Indians had little sympathy with the rebellion. The Madras army, largely low-caste men, had no common cause with the higher-caste, pampered soldiers of the Bengal army and little sympathy for them, and they were not slow to gain recruits, while many of the princes, like the Nizam of Hyderabad, an old friend of the British, who had long employed British soldiers in his forces, had held over 300,000 people in check who might otherwise have joined the rebels.

Even in Bengal and Oudh, with Lucknow's gallant defence, the grip had never been completely lost, and from the Punjab had come enormous strength. John Lawrence had not only held the country by sheer strength of character but had also dared to send away every able-bodied man he could spare to help win back Bengal, where the dissatisfied princes had hastened to take up their old power again

and landowners, thinking that the British rule was ended, had scrambled for what was going. The peasants, though for the most part in sympathy with the sepoys, obviously could not have resisted them and, though they sometimes murdered fugitives for what they could gain, they just as often saved English families, fed them and hid them, even to their own danger. Eighty years later alongside applications by their descendants for much sought-after jobs, well-folded, well-handled letters still appeared, which had been written by British women in extreme danger who had set down on paper the fact that this or that villager had saved her life.

In the end, only a small proportion of the population of 48 million had taken up arms, though it had been sufficient against the small numbers of the British and more than enough to reduce the whole of the Ganges valley and the surrounding countryside to chaos.

With Campbell's defeat of Tantia Topi and the Nana Sahib and the Gwalior mutineers, the main communication line along the river had held firm, and it was now important to open up contact with

Campbell brings the survivors of Lucknow to the bridge of boats across the river to burning Cawnpore.

the Punjab away in the north-west across Oudh, which lay athwart the route and was still aflame with rebellion. But now, just as the tide had turned along the Ganges, so it had also turned in Central India.

By October, when the garrison of Lucknow had been settling down to its second siege, it had become clear to Durand, the acting agent at Indore, that he would have to do something about those mutineers who had remained untroubled during the rainy season, the chief danger a force of 15,000 men at Mandisur with 18 guns under a Moghul prince, Firuz Shah, against whom he could raise only 1,500 men and nine guns. Moving against him on 22 October, he met a force of mercenaries who had been foolish enough to come into the open from the fort at Dhar, and drove them away, then, demolishing the fort, he followed the rebels towards Mandisur, defeating them near Mahidpur, though with heavy casualties on both sides. Turning and lashing out at another force at Goraria which he drove off after a hard battle, he found that Firuz Shah had escaped, so he headed for Indore where he disarmed the army of the state ruler. The agent, Sir Robert Hamilton, was now back in control and Durand handed over the men he had used so swiftly and   179 with such determination, and they became part of a new force, the Central India Field Force, which was given to Major-General Sir Hugh Rose, who had arrived in India in September.

This fine soldier was without a doubt the best the Mutiny threw up. A dashing man of quick decision, polished, dandified and gallant, he was considered by his officers at first to be effeminate and weak and unable to rough it much. They were about as inaccurate as it was possible to be because underneath the smooth exterior was a core of steel. Not having been in India before, his methods did not always recommend themselves to officers of the old school, but he had tremendous will power and energy and was the ideal commander for a series of flying columns designed to pursue a tough, slippery enemy. He believed in giving the rebels no rest and, taking up his command in December, he immediately dressed his men in khaki instead of red and, despite the casualties he suffered from battle and from disease, he was never once turned from his purpose, not even by Canning's hesitations, and his thousand-mile march to Kalpi and on to Gwalior in the summer heat of 1858 was considered by Fortescue, the historian of the British Army, to be the most remarkable achievement of the whole Mutiny. Yet, to their disgust, his men, because they were not involved in the sentimentalities of Cawnpore and Lucknow, received no special clasp or prize money while Rose himself remained – and has since remained – largely unnoticed.

British troops had been sent by now from Burma, Ceylon, Mauritius and Persia. Soldiers on the way to China had been turned back, while others had come – not very successfully – from the Crimea overland and from England by the Cape because the Suez Canal had not yet been constructed. It was decided to build up Campbell's forces for an all-out campaign, using the time until sufficient men arrived to clear the area between the Ganges and the Jumna. Transport was still short, however, because much of it had carried the survivors of Lucknow to Allahabad and was now out of reach, but Campbell made his first move on Christmas Eve and on 2 January, 1858, occupied the town and fort of Fatehgahr between Allahabad and Delhi. With the addition of a column from Delhi, bringing badly-needed transport, which he met at Bewar on the road to Fatehgarh, Campbell now had ten thousand men under his command and proposed to move into Rohilkhand after the rebels, using in addition to his own forces a contingent of Gurkhas from Nepal to the east. It was his wish to leave Oudh until later.

Concerned, however, that Oudh might become a rallying point for other disaffected provinces, Canning considered it should be

The Relief of Lucknow
  by George Jones.

The charge of the
2nd Dragoon Guards
at Lucknow.

tackled first. Though the legitimate king had remained a prisoner in Calcutta, the rebels had crowned one of his colourless minor sons in his place as a rallying point, with his mother, the Begum, exercising authority on his behalf. In addition, Outram, still waiting in the Alambagh, was being threatened by increasing numbers of rebels led by the Maulavi of Faizabad. He had been attacked again and again by forces always vastly outnumbering his own and had received only enough reinforcements to make up what he had lost as casualties.

Campbell, therefore, was ordered to return to Cawnpore but, while he waited for reinforcements for an assault on Oudh, he harassed the rebels as much as possible, deceiving the mutineers in Oudh into thinking he intended to launch an attack on Bareilly. A column was sent from Fatehgarh to give this impression and a threatening rebel force fifteen thousand strong stayed where it was. When they discovered they had been misled, an attack was mounted across the Ganges at Shamsabad, but was driven back into Rohilkhand. On 15 February 1858, Campbell himself left Fatehgarh for Cawnpore to make his final preparations for his advance into Oudh.

Sir Hugh Rose, meanwhile, was already performing the first of the military miracles that marked his campaign in Central India. Again and again he was to face vast rebel forces which could easily have overwhelmed him but with an insolent contempt for what could – and might well – happen, again and again he attacked them and put them to flight. Though he had only 4,500 men, most of them Indians, he immediately got on the move, despite the usual problems of transport and supplies. Moving from Mhow, he learned that 170 European women and children and a small European garrison of 68 artillerymen at Saugur were awaiting the arrival of a large body of mutineers whom it was firmly expected would be joined by the native troops there. He immediately changed direction but, as he attacked the fort of Rahatgarh en route, he was himself attacked by another rebel force under the Rajah of Banpur. He drove it off and took the fort, and another fight at Bina cleared the rebels from the area, and he arrived on 3 February 1858 at Saugur where the Europeans had been living in fear for eight long months.

Following his intention not to let the rebels rest, Rose now turned east and smashed a rebel-held fort at Gathakot, and swung towards Jhansi, which was a threat to the rear of Sir Colin Campbell. Plagued by the usual transport problems and the heat, on 4 March he feinted against one rebel-held pass at Malthon and sent in his main attack against another at Madanpur, the victory clearing a great deal of country of the rebels. By 20 February, his troops were fourteen miles from Jhansi, when he was ordered both by Campbell and Canning to the relief of two loyal rajahs besieged at Charkheri eighty miles away by Tantia Topi and the Gwalior Contingent. Deciding that the man on the spot knew better and that an attack where he was would draw off Tantia Topi, Rose, with the blessing of the agent, Sir Robert Hamilton, ignored the instruction and turned his attention to Jhansi.

By 23 February, Campbell was again across the Ganges and following Havelock's old route to Unao at a pace of 20 to 30 miles a day. With him now were about 20,000 men, and 54 heavy guns, eight light guns and mortars. As ever, the commissariat was badly organised and inefficient and, unlike Havelock's stripped-down force, this army was moulded in the old style, a vast winding procession, miles long, of creaking carts, guns, palanquins, litters, bullocks, pack horses, camels, elephants, tramping men, driven cattle for rations, and hordes of servants, stirring up a vast cloud of fine dust as they went and clearing the country of food and forage as if they had been locusts. Following them, Russell found halting places under trees full of broken earthenware and the whitened bones of cattle, and near Allahabad, under a grove of trees filled with green parrots, vultures and buzzards, he saw an array of tents with, behind them, more tents for servants, syces, grass-cutters and camel men, three horses, three camels, a pair of bullocks and a few goats. 'I was curious to know who this millionaire could be,' he said, but it turned out to be a mere captain of Irregulars travelling up-country with the usual train of home comforts.

Russell was still troubled by all the stories he had heard of atrocities. As he had moved up-country he had seen bodies hanging from trees, but though he saw scrawled messages on burned bungalows, 'Revenge your slaughtered countrywomen', he remained unimpressed; when he began to make enquiries, he found, 'No one could tell me of a single mutilation of any woman to which the could depose of their personal knowledge.'

When he reached Cawnpore he found little had even now been changed. Rows of gorged vultures sat on the crumbling parapets of Wheeler's entrenchment and the land around was covered with a fine, powdered dust two or three inches deep composed of sand, pulverised earth and the brick powder and mortar from ruined houses, which rose into the air on the slightest breeze.

The 72nd Highlanders
in Rajputana, showing
a detachment on camels.

The worst feature of the massacre was considered, it seemed to
him, not to be the fact that people had been killed but that 'the deed
was done by a subject race – by black men who dared to shed the
blood of their masters', and he discovered that the harrowing
phrases supposed to have been scrawled on the walls there by the
murdered victims which so inflamed the soldiers passing through –
'Remember the 15th of July, 1857 . . . Oh! My Child! My Child!
Countrymen, revenge!' and 'We are at the mercy of savages who
have ravished young and old' – had not been written at the time of
the atrocities but long afterwards.

The naval guns with Campbell were drawn by thirteen pairs of
oxen or by two elephants. Bullocks were preferred because they
caused no problems except crossing nullahs, rivers or sand, when
they all pulled different ways or not at all. They got their heads out

of the yokes, kicked, butted and gave all manner of trouble, while the gun sank and went on sinking, till it had to be pushed out by an elephant 'in the cleverest way', so that the bullocks could be made to renew their efforts and two hundred men on ropes could pull it out by main force. The elephants had one fault. 'In their wisdom,' it was noted, 'they dislike extremely going under fire, and if they are hit they become unmanageable.' They bolted off in panic, trumpeting, their trunks in the air, whereas bullocks advanced stolidly under the heaviest musketry and cannon fire with the utmost unconcern. The sailors appeared to puzzle the Indians. According to one of them, the rebels had thought the Highlanders were the spirits of murdered women, but the sailors astonished them. 'Four feet high, four feet broad, long hair and dragging big guns. They can't make them out.'

Against Campbell was an estimated force of 100,000 rebels determined to hang on to Lucknow. With the British out of the city, the rebel leaders had constructed three lines of defences, the first outside the city, the second and third centred on the major buildings which had proved such an obstacle in November. They had plenty of heavy artillery and the main streets had been barricaded and buildings loopholed and fortified. Fortunately, however, believing that Campbell would return by the same route as before, they had left the northern part of the city undefended, and Campbell's engineer, Napier, offered a plan which would send in the main body from the south with another part crossing the river to attack from the north.

On 2 March, Campbell seized the Dilkusha after a 'regular race' between the Sikhs and the Highlanders to catch the enemy. As the rebels streamed out, the Indian dhooly bearers trudged in behind the British to pick up the wounded, but, with enemy artillery hammering him, Campbell could not move his infantry until his own batteries were established. The next day, under their fire the enemy withdrew their guns and, with his line touching the river, Campbell began the building of two pontoon bridges. On 5 March, the Nepal Contingent arrived, swelling his force to 31,000 men and 104 guns.

By the evening of the 5th, the bridges were completed, and before daybreak the next day Outram's division was across the river and advancing up the far bank. By evening he was four miles from the city and half a mile from the scene of Lawrence's battle at Chinhut. On 9 March, an attack was started on the rebel left while, with the sun a hazy red ball in the sky, Outram began his attack from the north. The rebel shooting started, a 'zigzag fire of musketry' which went 'twitteringly along the lines of the trenches, like a long train of gunpowder.' Russell saw a gun drawn by three pairs of bullocks, 'a swell in a gilt palanquin', another dignitary on an elephant with a silver howdah and great umbrella, numerous well-mounted horsemen curvetting through the meadows and swarms of footmen, all in white with black cartouche boxes – 'formidable in all but organisation'. The operation was a complete success and Outram was able to join up with the attack against the left. Artillery was brought up to attack the Martinière College in the rear and to hold down the fire from the city.

Campbell had also moved forward and, launching an artillery and infantry attack on the Martinière, captured it with only a few casualties, among whom was Peel, of the naval brigade. With guns firing on them from both sides, the rebels now had to face Campbell's main attack. With Outram moving round from the north to attack an iron bridge leading across the river to the Residency and a stone bridge near the Machchi Bewan, Campbell had established himself on the city side of the canal so that he was able to fire on the Begum Kothi palace. Without opposition the Sikanderbagh – the dead of the November battle now only whitened bones picked clean by scavenging animals and birds – and the Shah Najaf mosque were occupied and the troops were sent in against the position at the Begum Kothi, which was believed to be held by five thousand men.

It was a confusing area of walls and courtyards but the garrison seemed unwilling to fight, though about seven hundred of them were killed. British casualties were small, one of the dead being William Hodson, the cavalryman who had shot the Moghul princes at Delhi. He had become a legend in his lifetime and troops fresh from England crowded round to see him whenever he appeared. He had twice been wounded since Delhi, once in the arm and once in the leg, but had not been able to resist being in at the death, and as they broke into the Begum's palace he was among the leaders. Still limping from his wound, he had driven up in a carriage but as Forbes-Mitchell, of the Highlanders, sent men off for gunpowder to blow in a door, he had rushed forward intending to lead an attack. Forbes-Mitchell had tried to stop him but he was too late and Hodson fell back, crying 'Oh, my wife!' and choking on his own blood as a bullet passed through his chest. He was taken to a building next door where he died in agony. He was said to have died while plundering. While this was denied, there is little doubt that he was heavily in debt and everyone knew he and his men did indulge in the practice. He also had a list of places where plunder was avail-

Opposite Jewelled Indian dagger and scabbard (*above*).

How Campbell's troops, on their last attack on Lucknow, found the Sikanderbagh. The remains of the rebels killed in the earlier attack after being ravaged by scavenging animals and birds.

able and with him was an orderly carrying a large haversack. He believed the room he was entering to contain treasure and, though he was not actually plundering when he died, there is little doubt that if he had lived another three minutes he would have been. He was a magnificent leader of irregular horse but a most unscrupulous man who had 'looked to the campaign to repair his fortunes'. As it happened, he left his wife little more than his sword and the fame of his regiment.

Others were certainly plundering. The marble pavement was inches deep in fragments of broken mirrors and chandeliers, and the men were still busy smashing everything the could find. In the Imambarra Mosque, there was not a space four yards square which did not bear the mark of shot or shell, and the courtyards were full of wreckage, fragments of sepoys' clothing, powder horns, firelocks, matchlocks, shields and tulwars.

Mining, blasting and artillery operations carried the British nearer their goal and by 14 March the heavy artillery was tearing holes in the thick masonry of the Kaisarbagh. A palace overlooking it was occupied and fire directed against the rebel artillery which was abandoned. It had been intended at this point to halt and continue by mining but the Sikhs and a few of the 10th Foot continued and managed to turn the rebel defence line. As the rebels began to withdraw, every available man was pushed forward to reinforce them. They went in yelling 'Revenge for the death of Hodson.'

The sun was setting by this time but there was no calm in the evening air. Dropping shots never ceased and the noise of the plunderers was heard in all directions. A terrified Kashmiri boy leading an aged blind man flung himself begging for mercy at the feet of an officer of the Bengal Fusiliers who, to the disgust of his men, drew his revolver. Three times his revolver misfired, his men crying 'Shame' each time, but on the fourth attempt he succeeded in shooting the boy through the head.

Enthusiasm was so high it was decided an attempt should be made on the Kaisarbagh itself. The rebels seemed curiously unconcerned and kites were seen floating in the sky over the garden but the British knew, as Russell said, that any one of the amiable kite-flyers would happily disembowel them if they caught them, and troops were brought up from the Sikanderbagh and the Shah Najaf mosque and soon all the rebel strongpoints round the Kaisarbagh were captured and the Kaisarbagh isolated. It was soon captured and, as the rebels inside were shot down, the soldiers again went mad in an orgy of plundering, throwing out embroidered cloths, silver vessels, instruments, pictures, standards and weapons. Drunk with excitement, they smashed everything they could lay their hands on and burned what they couldn't smash in a fire in the courtyard. There was perhaps some excuse. They had fought all day in the steamy heat, surrounded by rotting corpses, driving forward in a frenzy of excitement from which they could not be snatched at a moment's notice, and British and native soldiery, moving through the vast courts, were still firing from among statues, lamp-posts and orange trees at mutineers. Windows and panels were shattered and there were dead and dying sepoys among the orange groves and sprawled among the flowers. White statues were reddened with blood and, leaning against a smiling Venus, a British soldier shot through the neck was gasping out his life.

Since bags of gunpowder attached to slow matches had been

thrown into rooms containing stubborn rebels, many of the wounded and hundreds of the bodies were half-burned and the stench was appalling. Russell watched as officers tried in vain to control their men but soldiers laden with shawls, tapestries, gold and silver brocade, caskets of jewels, arms and dresses, wild with fury and lust for gold – 'literally drunk with plunder' – were smashing china vases and mirrors, gouging precious stones from the stems of pipes, saddlecloths and firearms, even carrying off useless brass pots, pictures and vases of jade. The Kaisarbagh storehouses were full of wooden cases jammed with china, bowls, goblets, and hookahs, and soldiers like banditti, their faces black with powder, their coats stuffed with valuables, appeared and reappeared in a scene of indescribable plunder, moving about through endless courts as stifling as vapour baths, and past scenes 'worthy of the Inferno'. There were blazing walls which might contain mines, deadly smells and clouds of offensive flies which rose from corpses bloated by the appalling heat, as the camp followers, 'foul as vultures', joined in the search for loot.

Terrified female members of the royal family were found cowering in a large, low, dark, dirty room without windows, and by the evening the city was virtually in Campbell's hands. But, because of a strange and mistaken last-minute order from him which had held Outram back when he was about to capture the iron bridge which lay along their route to safety, the rebels were able to stream away unhindered. Among them were the rebel leaders, Firuz Shah, Kunwar Singh, and the Begum with the boy king. By another mistake, the rebel leaders still in the city also escaped because Campbell then sent his cavalry after the fugitives. According to Lord Roberts, the campaign should have ended there and then but, because of these errors, it was to drag on for another year, as the fugitives spread across Oudh, occupying one strong position after another.

The following day was spent in consolidating and, on 16 March, Outram was ordered to storm the Residency he had not long before been defending. This time the siege lasted only half an hour then the defenders took to their heels. Small battles continued round the perimeter of the area held by the British but were all driven off and, on 18 March, learning that the Begum of Oudh and the young king were at the Musabagh, a country palace four miles away, Outram was ordered to advance on it while Hope Grant bombarded it and Brigadier Campbell took up a position to intercept fugitives. As Outram opened fire the rebels fled but, due to a mistake by Brigadier Campbell, who claimed he had lost his way, they were again allowed to escape. The Maulavi of Faizabad was still in

View of the Residency area after the third siege.

Lucknow, barricaded in a building with two guns and, though his position was also assaulted, he too escaped.

As Havelock's son said, 'Our magnificent force was capable of crushing everything: it could overtake nothing.' Campbell never fully understood the conditions of success in Indian warfare and, as he took time to assemble large bodies of troops, his movements became too slow. Unlike Rose, he also had an unnecessary respect for his enemy, and they did not hesitate to take advantage of his methods. Cautious and intensely conservative by disposition, he turned down Havelock's suggestion of a corps of mounted infantry and by his failure of judgement allowed over 100,000 rebels to get away from Lucknow.

By the 23rd, the last of them had gone. The British losses had been small – 127 officers and men killed and 595 wounded – compared with the vast numbers at Delhi. Unfortunately, many of those whose lives had been saved died later in the hot weather campaigns against the rebels who had been allowed to escape, when only 100 were killed in action against over 1,000 who perished from heat-stroke and disease.

Chapter 12

The End
of Rebellion

With Lucknow at last firmly in British hands, the task of pacifying the countryside began. There was a growing confidence in the air and, with the deep interest in the Mutiny that was manifested in the English newspapers that arrived, those women who had kept diaries at Delhi or during the siege of Lucknow realised they had something of interest to offer and were beginning to consider publication. Refugees who had been hiding for months began to turn up, however, sick and ill, everything they possessed gone, their families dead or scattered. Russell saw two Eurasian girls, a drummer's daughters, neither of them sixteen years old, who had been carried off by mutineers. As Russell delicately put it, they had 'escaped worse than death by . . . compliance with the worst'. Despite the torment they had suffered, they still had to complain of the rudeness of aloof British officers.

The stamping out of the revolt was still to take a long time. Clearly there could be no coming to terms with men who had committed that most heinous of military crimes, mutiny, and a proclamation by Canning that the land of anyone who had been in rebellion against the British was to be forfeited became, in effect, an announcement of war to the death. In addition, Havelock's early failures to reach Lucknow and Campbell's abandonment of it after the second relief only served to encourage the rebels.

Still hampered by a shortage of men, Rose had been busy in Central India, however. Jhansi had proved a tough nut to crack with a strong fort which could not be attacked without first subduing the city. After a long bombardment, he was about to storm the place when, on 31 March, he learned that Tantia Topi had arrived as he had expected. He had just captured Charkheri when he had received a message from the Rani of Jhansi demanding help. With him he had 22,000 men and 28 guns.

Faced by one of the mutineers' best leaders, Rose did not even bother to raise the siege and detached only a portion of his force, consisting of less than 2,000 men, only a third of whom were British. It was his intention to attack on 1 April, but he was forestalled by Tantia Topi's own attack. A report that another column was advancing on the River Betwa to relieve Jhansi had drawn off more of Rose's troops and he now had barely 1,000 men but he threw back Tantia's flanks with artillery and cavalry and drove in his centre with the British infantry. Tantia Topi fled to Kalpi, leaving behind all his guns, stores and equipment.

While this battle had been going on, the bombardment of Jhansi had continued and two days later Rose feinted against the west wall

Opposite
The capture of
Tantia Topi.

195

while he threw his main attack at the opposite side. After a bloody
battle, the place fell, with no mercy given to the rebels, and in the
street fighting which followed rebels who could not escape threw
their wives and children into wells and then jumped in themselves.
The streets were choked with corpses by this time, and as the
soldiers collected them by the hundred and set fire to them, the air
stank with the odour of burning flesh and it became difficult to
breathe. With men groaning from wounds or from fearful burns
where they had been trapped in blazing rooms, and all suffering
from the frightful heat, many were calling hysterically for water
among the ruins. But, anxious to destroy the city as a symbol of
cruelty, not a scrap of pity was shown by the British, though the one
person they had hoped to capture was gone. The Rani, whom they
held responsible for the slaughter of the British residents, had taken
advantage of the besiegers' concern for loot and killing and, after
fighting with her troops, she had stolen out of the fort with a few
attendants, dressed as a man. The victory was complete, however,
and thousands of rebels had been killed, many of them after the fall
of the city. The British had lost just over three hundred. Rose had
been lucky but his courage had paid off.

Changing his views, Canning had now decided that Oudh could
be left for the time being after all while Rohilkhand, which Campbell
had been about to attack at the beginning of the year, should be
occupied. So, leaving Hope Grant to garrison Lucknow, Campbell
began to send out columns to fight small isolated battles – at Bari
against the Maulavi of Faizabad, and at Azamgarh, where a small
196   British force was besieged after a new rising by Kunwar Singh.

Both these men, among the best of the rebel leaders, were defeated. The Maulavi was driven into Rohilkhand and Kunwar Singh, old and ill and with his stronghold at Jagdishpur destroyed, was trying to cross the Ganges. He had indifferently lopped off a hand shattered by a cannon ball and thrown it into the sacred water of the river as his last offering but, although he was dying, he was still able to turn round and smash a British force sent against him from Arrah in another defeat as decisive as Chinhut.

While Kunwar Singh was fighting his last battle, the energetic Rose, leaving a small force at Jhansi, turned his attention on Kalpi, where a rebel force under the Rao Sahib, the Nana Sahib's nephew and another excellent leader – now joined by the Rani of Jhansi – threatened Campbell's rear. Held back by the exhaustion of his men after continuous fighting in the heat of the Indian sun, he sent off the first of his forces on 22 April. A plan to meet him offered by the Rani, a shrewd woman with a great grasp of military tactics, was not used and Tantia Topi, a good but slipshod leader, chose a position at Kunch where he once again concentrated too much on his centre and left his flanks unguarded. Rose, who was well served by his intelligence service, again decided to attack the flanks and the battle was over in an hour, the rebels losing 600 men against Rose's 62.

His men suffering from exhaustion and heatstroke, Rose, who was himself having cold water poured over him regularly to keep him from fainting in the heat, was unable to follow up his victory, but he was determined to finish the rebels off before the rains came, and by the middle of May he was only six miles from Kalpi. The heat was such, however, that it mummified the dead, and dhooly after dhooly went to the rear containing white men laughing or sobbing with the hysteria of heatstroke, while even half the native troops under his command were affected by it. The rebels, in fact, made a practice of deliberately holding back their attacks until the heat of the sun was able to help them.

The force at Kalpi, alarmed at first, had now been reinforced, however, by the Nawab of Banda, a relative of the Rao Sahib, and by other scattered units. They had chosen a good position based on broken country, the river, and a line of walled temples. Unfortunately, they assumed as usual that Rose would make a frontal attack. Rose was far too crafty, however, and with most of his staff sick and the heat rising to 117 degrees, he prepared for battle. On 22 May, waiting until the sun was high, the rebels were the first to attack. Their feint against his left did not fool Rose, but the British had been decimated by heatstroke and, with the remainder of them 197 weak, they were forced to retire. As the rebels broke through almost to his tents, Rose was saved by cavalry mounted on camels and he drove them back on his left to cut off a portion of their forces. There was a pause during the night when some of those struck down by the sun were able to recover but by dawn the next day the rebels, well aware of Rose's reputation, had fled and he found he had captured one of their ordnance factories and arsenals, as well as trophies from Windham's defeat at Cawnpore.

While Rose was smashing every rebel attempt to stand within reach, Campbell, nicknamed 'Old-Be-Careful', had been moving warily. He was facing a considerable force of mutineers who had been joined by the Maulavi of Faizabad, but, razing the jungles to deprive the rebels of hiding places and to allow themselves clear fields of fire, a column left Lucknow on 7 April to clear the left bank of the Ganges. This should have been an easy task but its commander, through sheer incompetence, made a botch of an attack on a small fort at Ruya and came within an inch of disaster. That the rebels were by no means crushed was again shown soon afterwards when General Penny with another column was killed in an ambush at Kukerauli – chiefly due to his own carelessness.

It had been expected by Campbell that he would meet the rebels himself at Shahjahanpur, but they had already fled and the Maulavi of Faizabad had escaped once more. Leaving a small garrison, Campbell moved on towards Bareilly. As he advanced, the waiting rebels' first line fled without making any resistance but a group of Rohilla ghazis, fanatical Muslims wearing green turbans and cummerbunds and signet rings engraved with a text from the Koran, made a furious charge, dragging officers from their horses in a desperate fight. Russell, sick and ill after being kicked by his horse, was caught up in the middle of it. Tortured by flies, smothered in dust, prostrated by the heat and suffering from the loss of blood and the application of leeches, he was in a dhooly as the attack swept over him.

His bearers fled in terror and, in the middle of the panic, surrounded by trumpeting elephants and the screaming of women and children, he saw camp followers falling with cleft skulls and bleeding wounds. Helped into a saddle by his syce and wearing nothing but a shirt, he fled at full speed. Near him a camel driver, trying to protect his head, had his arms lopped off and his skull split open to the nose with a stroke of a razor-sharp tulwar, but as the ghazis advanced on him, by the grace of God he fainted and fell from his horse, and they thundered over him, leaving him untouched except for bruises. By the end of the struggle, in which they made no attempt to escape, every one of the ghazis was killed. Campbell, wary as ever and concerned to rest his troops in the heat of the day, once more allowed the remainder of the rebels to escape.

That night in unbelievable heat a storm broke, with hot strong winds, clouds of dust, lightning, whirling black clouds and a roaring sound through the trees like 'the hoofs of myriads of cavalry'. In empty Bareilly a general order was found. 'Do not attempt to meet the regular columns of the infidels,' it ran, 'because they are superior to you in discipline and bunderbust . . . but watch their movements . . . intercept their communications . . . stop their supplies . . . and keep constantly hanging about their camps.' The rebels were growing cunning.

As the British moved out, the heat and the storms continued and men dropped out right and left from the line of march. Still in his dhooly, Russell found an old soldier of the 80th alongside him gasping for breath during one of the halts. 'I've been 18 years in the service,' he said, 'and never had such hardship as this.' As the column reformed he was found to be dead.

It was becoming clear that Campbell was being out-manoeuvred all the time by the more swiftly-moving rebels. The force he had left at Shahjahanpur was attacked and an attempt at relief went wrong. In an attempt to relieve the relieving force, once again the Maulavi was allowed to escape. This was his last effort, however, and soon afterwards he was murdered by an Indian nobleman who, sensing that the British were winning, turned his coat. The Maulavi had always been among the most ardent of the rebel leaders and had constantly outwitted the British commanders.

The last flicker of fighting fell to Rose. Believing that the campaign was over, Campbell ordered the breaking up of the Central India Force and Rose had already said goodbye to his troops when news came of a new outbreak which might well have set the whole of Central India ablaze again. Tantia Topi had made an attack on Gwalior, the stronghold of the Maharajah Scindiah. A Mahratta ruling a country of Jats, the Maharajah had thrown in his lot with the British who he felt could help him hold his state, but Tantia Topi, though he had not managed to persuade him to change sides, had won over his army and his nobles. Believing the rebels disunited after their defeats by Rose, the Maharajah had marched out on 1 June to give battle but, with Tantia Topi, the Rani of Jhansi and the Rao Sahib, all intelligent leaders, against him, he was inevitably defeated and, as his troops went over to the rebels, he had to flee for his life while the rebels occupied Gwalior and proclaimed the Nana Sahib the ruler.

Fortunately for Rose, they wasted their time celebrating their victory and, instead of waiting for his relief, Rose resumed command, knowing that with the rains about to arrive, there wasn't a moment to lose. Inspired by his spirited leadership, his troops were more than willing to follow him and, joined by troops which Campbell had sent him, he moved north-west towards Gwalior where he was overtaken at Morar on 12 June, by Napier, his successor, who agreed to waive his right to command.

Although his force was exhausted by the long march, Rose drove the rebels back on 16 June, and on the following day, a force from Rajputana, hurrying to his assistance, met the rebels under the Rani of Jhansi at Kotah-ke-serai and drove them towards Gwalior. In the fight the Rani – 'the best and bravest military leader of the rebels', in Rose's opinion – was killed. She had been riding with the cavalry dressed in male attire and, struck in the side by a bullet, had kept her saddle only for a few seconds before falling from it, dead.

Exhausted by the heat, the triumphant troops were again unable to follow up their victory and the following day they were reinforced by Rose who, leaving Napier at Morar to watch for retreating rebels, marched on Gwalior. Cutting off a rebel force attempting to bring reinforcements, he had soon occupied the city. The Rao Sahib and Tantia Topi, however, had escaped once again.

The Central Indian campaign had ended, but Tantia Topi was not defeated. Though deserted by the Rao Sahib, he was now rallying forces near Jaipur. In heavy rain, he was caught up at Sanganir on 5 August, and driven away, and again the following day at Kotra, when again he escaped. Arriving at Jhalrapatan he collected guns, ammunition and a heavy ransom from the Rajah, and headed for Indore. But British forces were converging on him now, despite the heavy rains and he was defeated again at Mangrauli on 10 October. As usual, because of exhaustion and lack of cavalry, the British had to allow him to get away. Moving into Nagpur, however, he found it had turned against him because it was obvious by now that the British were putting down the rebellion, and he was again defeated at Chota Udaipur. At Nahergarh, he was joined by Man Singh, a Rajput chief and a relative of the Maharajah of Gwalior who had risen against the Maharajah, not because of a quarrel with the British but because he considered he had been robbed of his rights to the state of Narwar. With rebellion in the air,

The hill fortress
of Gwalior.

however, the British could not make distinctions and he and his
forces had been defeated and driven off.

The two men were joined by Firuz Shah, who had been driven
from Rohilkhand by Campbell. Between them now, though, they
could raise only two thousand desperate men. But with the British
all round them, they still managed to escape, and though caught
again at Daosa in the first days of 1859, again they slipped through
the net. They were caught again a week later at Sikar in Jaipur, but
once again escaped.

Separating and without supporters, they headed for the jungle,
and, with an amnesty by this time in force, on 7 April 1859,
almost two years since the first outbreak at Meerut, Man Singh
betrayed the whereabouts of Tantia Topi, who was captured,
alone and almost penniless, while he was asleep. At his trial, he
claimed he had only obeyed the orders of the Nana Sahib or the
Rao Sahib. He was hanged on the 18th, behaving with courage and
even adjusting the noose round his neck. The Rao Sahib was not
found until 1862, when he was also hanged. Firuz Shah managed
to reach Mecca, where he died penniless, in 1877. But by then the
Mutiny had been long over. It had died with Tantia Topi, the one
man who might have continued to raise a rebel force.

With the Mutiny and the rebellion it had provoked ended, the
British looked about them to see what they could do to prevent
another. There was no special section of the community which was
seen to be guilty. There had been Sikhs inside Delhi and fighting on
the Ridge, and while frontier tribesmen had enlisted on the British

side they had also been among the rebels in the north. Both Hindus and Muslims had been involved, and while some princes had fought for the British their brothers had often supported the rebels. Despite the attitude of the ordinary English soldiery it had never been a war of white against black, because in almost every English camp the British had been outnumbered by their Indian troops and would never have survived but for their Indian camp followers.

The Mutiny had laid waste vast areas on both sides of the Ganges valleys and had cost 40 million pounds and the lives of 2,034 soldiers in action and another 8,987 from disease or heatstroke, to say nothing of the murdered civilians and the thousands on thousands of native casualties. A few reputations, like Rose's and Hope Grant's and Campbell's, had been made, but many had been shattered and very few of the commanders of mutinous troops were re-appointed.

It was a time for restoring order. The amnesty proved to be of only short duration and the Nana Sahib, after an attempt to negotiate, disappeared, while the old Moghul king of Delhi died in exile. Hundreds of other Indians, many of them simple men whose only wish had been to avoid trouble, were hanged. As one man accused of desertion said, 'Where was I to go? All the world said the English Raj had come to an end and . . . being a quiet man, I thought the best place to take refuge was in my own home.' For years afterwards it was the habit of British writers to portray Indians as treacherous and unreliable, while their culture remained neglected and scorned, the contemplative qualities of Hinduism regarded as unmanly.

Russell wrote: 'I could not help thinking how harsh the reins of our rule must feel . . . The smallest English official treats their prejudices with contempt . . . Lord Clyde (Campbell) and others . . . were often pained by the insolence and rudeness of some of the civilians to the sirdars and chiefs in the north-west.' They demanded the cruellest punishments and apparently revelled in watching them. On one occasion two Englishwomen, who had turned up to watch rebels blown from guns, rode away with their white clothing scarlet and their horses shining with blood. Russell was shocked at the things that were done, feeling they would ultimately recoil on the British, and many officers told him that the worst effect was the destruction of confidence which the natives formerly felt in British justice.

With conditions beginning to return to normal, the old arrogant trust was soon back. Near Cawnpore, where the worst of the Indian outrages had occurred and where the British reprisals might have been expected to stir up the deepest feelings of hatred, Russell met a man going out to shoot. There were still rebels about in the hills but he was taking only a few Indian servants with him, confident that they would protect him.

'Can you trust them, after what has happened?' Russell asked.

'Well . . . they carry my guns . . . but they wouldn't do me any harm,' he was told.

'But what is the difference between them and sepoys?' Russell persisted.

The huntsman's reply was airily confident. 'Well,' he said, 'they're all niggers, but I *can* trust my fellows.'

However, the British did try to learn by their mistakes. The policy of annexation was dropped and every attempt was made to keep the princes on their side. It was also made clear that no interference with the Indian religions was to be allowed. The Indian Army was permitted to survive, but the differences in pay and prospects were not put right, and it was not until World War I that an Indian could hope to hold a commission. The biggest change that the Mutiny brought was that power to rule India was taken from the East India Company and given to the British Crown; nobody seemed to notice that the old prophecy that its power would crumble and disappear in 1857 had proved correct, after all. Though the rebels had been defeated and hundreds had lost their lives in defeating them, the rule of the Company had vanished with the first shots fired at Meerut.

The royal proclamation was read out at every station in India at the end of 1858. Military salutes, concerts, displays of bunting, banquets, illuminations, fireworks and, of course, religious services 'testified to the enthusiasm of the Europeans', while 'loyal addresses were signed by thousands of natives'. Whether they signed to protect themselves or their treasures or businesses or because they felt a genuine loyalty to the British was not clear.

The change brought one final flicker of outrage. The Company's locally-recruited white troops, when they found they had become soldiers of the Queen, found also that they could neither take their discharge nor claim a bounty for being re-enlisted in the Queen's forces. Rose, now Commander-in-Chief, handled it firmly, and it was decided that white troops in future would always come from England, that the native troops should never again outnumber the British by more than two to one, and that the artillery should always remain British. The four great lessons of the Mutiny were well learned: the necessity for preserving the prestige and authority of the regimental commanding officers; the necessity for keeping officers with their units and not allowing them to seek better 203 careers in the civil service; the necessity to see that class differences were not diluted; and that arsenals shouid always remain in European hands.

Though India was quiet again, after the Mutiny it would always remain a question mark. Despite its pride of place in the Empire, the British, for all their outward confidence, for all their apparent strength, never slept as soundly in their beds again. The fear of another rebellion was never far from their thoughts and, beneath the ostensible security, the feeling persisted until the day when the sub-continent was granted the privilege of self-rule.

Casualties of the war
in the hills.

Select Bibliography

Adye, Sir John: *Recollections of a Military Life*, London 1895
Collier, Richard: *The Sound of Fury*, London 1963
Cork, B. J.: *Rider on a Grey Horse*, London 1958
Edwardes, Michael, *Battles of the Indian Mutiny*, London, 1963
Ewart, Lt.-Gen. J. A.: *The Story of a Soldier's Life*, London 1881
Forbes-Mitchell, W.: *The Relief of Lucknow*, London, 1962
Germon, Maria: *Journal of the Siege of Lucknow*, London 1958
Gough, Sir Hugh: *Old Memories*, London 1897
Gowing, Timothy: *A Voice From The Ranks*, London 1905
Griffiths, Charles: *A Narrative of the Siege of Delhi*, London 1910
Hilton, Maj.-Gen. R.: *The Indian Mutiny*, London 1957
Holmes, T. Rice: *The Indian Mutiny*, London 1904
Joyce, Michael: *Ordeal at Lucknow*, London 1938
Kaye, J. W.: *History of the Sepoy War*, London 1880
Leasor, James: *The Red Fort*, London 1956
McMunn, Lt.-Gen. Sir G.: *The Indian Mutiny In Perspective*, London 1931
Malleson, Col. G. B.: *The Indian Mutiny of 1857*, London 1912
Muter, Mrs Dunbar: *My Recollections of the Sepoy Revolt*, London 1911
Pearson, Hesketh: *The Hero of Delhi*, London 1939
Roberts, Field-Marshal Lord: *Forty-One Years in India*, London 1897
Russell, W. H.: *My Indian Mutiny Diary*, London 1951
Sen, Surendra Nath: *Eighteen Fifty-Seven*, London 1957
Sylvester, J. H. (Ed A. McK. Annand): *Cavalry Surgeon*, London 1971
Tisdall, E. E. P.: *Mrs. Duberly's Campaigns*, London 1963
Verney, Maj.-Gen. G. L.: *The Devil's Wind*, London 1956
Wolseley, Viscount: *The Story of a Soldier's Life*, London 1903
Woodruffe, Philip: *The Men Who Ruled India*. Vol 1, London 1965

Index

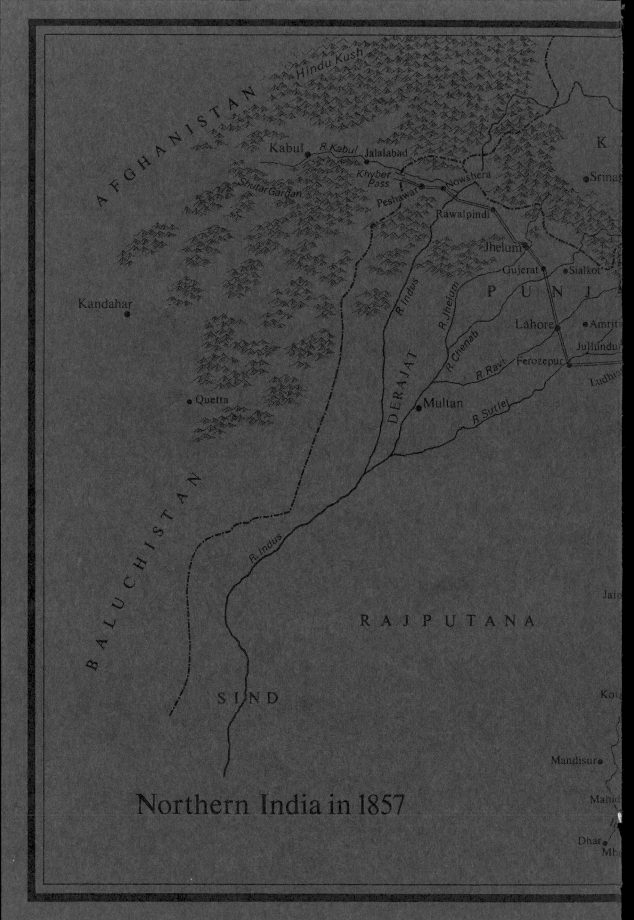

Northern India in 1857